Servants on the Move

Servants on the Move

Employers' Race-Gender Ideology and Service Work on Trains, Planes, and Cruise Ships

Francisca E. Oyogoa

LEXINGTON BOOKS
Lanham • Boulder • New York • London

Published by Lexington Books
An imprint of The Rowman & Littlefield Publishing Group, Inc.
4501 Forbes Boulevard, Suite 200, Lanham, Maryland 20706
www.rowman.com

86-90 Paul Street, London EC2A 4NE

British Library Cataloguing in Publication Information Available

Library of Congress Cataloging-in-Publication Data

Names: Oyogoa, Francisca E., author.
Title: Servants on the move : employers' race-gender ideology and service work on trains, planes, and cruise ships / Francisca E. Oyogoa.
Description: Lanham : Lexington Books, [2024] | Includes bibliographical references and index. | Summary: "This book examines employers' role in creating, upholding, and legitimating race-gender inequality on trains, planes, and cruise ships and focuses on employer's actions and statements related to racial and gender hierarchies among their workers"—Provided by publisher.
Identifiers: LCCN 2024019023 | ISBN 9781666954708 (cloth) | ISBN 9781666954715 (ebook)
Subjects: LCSH: Pullman porters. | Women, White—Employment. | Flight attendants. | Cruise ships—Employees. | Employees—Travel. | Minorities—Employment. | Equality.
Classification: LCC HD8039.S45 O96 2024 | DDC 331.7/93—dc23/eng/20240528
LC record available at https://lccn.loc.gov/2024019023

Dedicated to:
Tony
Mom
Kevin
Dan Clawson
All the workers, past and present, who reside at the proverbial "bottom of the boat"

Contents

Figures ix

Tables xi

Acknowledgments xiii

1 The World They Created 1

2 The Origins of Service Workers in the Pullman Railroad Company, 1858–1880s 19

3 Pullman Executives' Public and Private Racial Discourse, 1890s–1950s 39

4 White Femininity Takes Flight, 1910s–1970s 67

5 Going Global: Service Work, Race-Gender-Nationality on Cruise Ships: 1970–2000s 97

6 Conclusion: Some Things Change, Others Stay the Same 115

References 123

Index 133

About the Author 139

Figures

2.1	Porters Serving Passengers in Railway Car 1882	28
2.2	Porters Working in the Pullman Car Kitchen	29
3.1	An Innocent Abroad	45
3.2	The World's Most Perfect Servant	47
3.3	A Fair Lady in Her Sleeper	49
3.4	Behold Porter J. Henry Smith	54
3.5	Porter Glasgow Carries White Toddler	58
3.6	Porter Glasgow in Juvenile Parade	59
3.7	Porter with White Baby	59
4.1	Bessie Coleman, Aviatrix	71
4.2	Flight Attendant Serving a Meal	84
4.3	TWA Stewardesses in Front of Plane	84
4.4	Pre-Flight Stewardess Responsibilities	85
4.5	1960s Flight Attendant	92

Tables

2.1 Illinois and Chicago Population in 1860 34
2.2 Illinois and Chicago Population in 1870 34
3.1 1915 Monthly Wage Schedule for Conductors and Porters 42
3.2 Monthly Pensions of Pullman Employees, 1904 44
3.3 Pullman Company Charitable Donations, 1897–1913 50
5.1 Salaries/Vacation for Select Ship Positions 107

Acknowledgments

This book could not have been completed without the guidance, love, and support of many people. My deepest gratitude goes to my dissertation committee and especially to my advisor and mentor, the late Dan Clawson, for his wisdom, steadfastness, and inspiration. I am deeply indebted to an anonymous reviewer and Chris Tilly for their constructive suggestions. My friend Nancy, you were the only person I trusted to read the first draft of the book and truly understand what I was aiming to accomplish in this work; your unabashed encouragement and enthusiasm heartened me greatly; thank you so much. The research contained in this book was funded in part by the University of Massachusetts Graduate School, the Social Science Research Council, the Woodrow Wilson Fellowship Foundation, the American Philosophical Society, and the Bard College at Simon's Rock faculty fund. The staff at the Newberry Library were accommodating, and the folks at the Meriden Public Library created a communal space necessary to mitigate the solitude of writing.

I am fortunate to work in two unique spaces, surrounded by supportive colleagues and friends in the faculty, staff, and administration. Bard Holyoke is the only place I want to be on a Monday morning because of all the fantastic women who inhabit that space. You all bring so much joy, knowledge, and laughter into my life. A special thanks to Simon's Rock for giving me the time and space to finish this book. Simon's Rock is an entire community of faculty, staff, and students who have made our intimate space a home I cherish. There are genuinely too many friends on campus to name, but you know who you are. As for the many exceptional students I have worked with over these years, understand that if you feel I have positively impacted your life, trust that you have done the same for me.

I would also like to thank my family and friends for their emotional support and encouragement; I could not have finished without you. Special thanks to my Aunt Hazel and Uncle Michael for a lifetime of laughter and unconditional love. Karen, Ed, Kelly, and Margaret—you are the best in-laws anyone could ever ask for, and I cherish all of you. I am blessed to call the Agees, Darlings, Foremans, Gradys, Jacksons, Ogunsanyas, and Surowieckis family. As for Ryan and Braden, my nephews who have grown up to be young men I adore. We are no longer the "three musketeers" making up songs about how "cookies make us big and strong," but you will forever be two of my favorite and most beloved humans. Whether snow tubing, ziplining, dunking at the trampoline park, or just hanging out—our time together has always brought me immeasurable joy, even during some of the most challenging times in my life; thank you. I am eternally grateful to Jasmin for being my best friend, confidant, and "ride or die" for all these years. To my squad—Eden-Renee, Kristy, Manat, and Cristina—your friendship and encouragement have sustained me, and I could not have finished this book without all of you.

Anthony and Mom, because of you, I have been allowed to build a life that "suits the fashion of my soul," as Du Bois would say. You both inspire me, and I am truly blessed that we have only grown closer over the years. Everything good in my life started with both of you. Finally, I would like to thank Kevin. You have been by my side throughout this journey, always there with friendship, love, support, nurturing, care, and unrelenting laughter. You cheered me on from start to finish and consistently demonstrated why choosing you was my best decision ever.

Chapter 1

The World They Created

What explains racial and gender inequality in the workplace? Indeed, understanding the origins and causes of hierarchies is integral to finding solutions. This book approaches the issue of race-gender workplace inequality by using firm-level data from railroad, airline, and cruise ship companies. The central questions addressed are: Why and how did race-gender hierarchies get created, maintained, legitimized, and challenged on trains, airplanes, and cruise ships?

During the eras covered, workers on trains, planes, and cruise ships worked in what we might term the "entertainment-service-transport sector." In these instances, more than the mere conveyance from one location to another is being purchased. Employers encourage customers to feel entitled to a mixture of amusement, congeniality, attentiveness, servility, food service, and being cleaned up afterward. Employers in these contexts depend on the performance of specific types of interactions between customers and employees. These interactions are shaped by prevailing or newly constructed race-gender norms and the nature of the job (e.g., wages, tenure, and benefits). This book is based on the premise that capitalism is not a system with an "invisible hand" that works independently of actual human beings who are socialized in a specific time and place. Capitalism is a set of power relations imposed on and contested by different individuals and groups.

In the United States, elite White men have played an outsized role in shaping the discursive terrain and hoarding opportunities for themselves (Ducey and Feagin 2017). All three cases and time periods examined—Pullman Railroad Company (1866 to 1965), the four major U.S. airlines (1930 to 1970s), and U.S.-owned cruise companies (1970s to 2013)—are instances where ownership and upper management were *all* White men. The "hegemony of White masculinity" was irrefutable. In this definition, the "hegemony of White masculinity" refers to a workplace structure where White men maintain an elevated status and possess the exclusive right to compel obedience, deference, and subservience from other workers, including people of color and White women. Essential to hegemonic White masculinity is that work was *never* structured in a way that necessitated White men being placed in an inferior position to anyone other than another White male.

In all three instances, company executives consciously decided to create a work environment that was hierarchically segregated along race and gender lines. Once capitalists and their agents in management decided to typecast a new job as "best suited" for one group of people (i.e., Black men on trains, White women on planes), they would maintain these hiring practices for decades even when qualified, cheaper, and more proximate labor outside the designated group was readily available.

In addition to creating the structure of race-gender segregation, company executives spent vast amounts of money teaching, policing, and advertising these ostensibly "innate" human differences. Specifically, the racial and gender identity of workers was inscribed on the occupation in multiple ways, such as pre-employment training, employee rulebooks, company newsletters, recruitment ads, hiring and firing practices, disciplinary actions, and well-publicized advertising campaigns in popular culture. In both practice and cultural representations, being a porter became synonymous with Black manhood, and the flight attendant was an exemplar of White femininity. Upper management insisted that gendered racialization be embodied and repeatedly performed. The aim was for workers to appear "naturally" cheerful and inclined toward servitude. Notably, this ostensibly natural behavior was only manufactured after rigorous training, repeated instruction, and mastery of detailed rulebooks with dozens of specific requirements. Company records demonstrate that executives relied on diverse race-gender ideologies to justify why each group was innately "best suited" for certain types of work. Workers' identities ultimately shaped job requirements, customer expectations, and what employers deemed fair working conditions and pay.

Employers' race-gender ideology is a causal agent for racial and gender hierarchies among workers. However, multiple factors, various theoretical perspectives, and competing explanations exist for these unequal outcomes. An overview of critical works and perspectives addressing these issues will be discussed next.

This section overviews some prevailing explanations for race-gender inequality among workers. We begin with a discussion of the role White male workers play in excluding women and workers of color from their occupations. Next, we shift our attention to some key frameworks focusing on the actions of employers, in this instance, White male employers, who play a role in creating occupational hierarchies that discriminate against all women and people of color.

WHITE WORKERS MARGINALIZE THEIR BLACK COUNTERPARTS

Edna Bonacich's "split labor market theory" remains one of the most important contributions to our understanding of race and work. Bonacich argues that between World War I and the New Deal, White workers actively sought to marginalize Black workers (Bonacich 1976). White workers engaged in militant trade unionism and strikes to improve their working conditions. To undermine White workers' militancy, employers began hiring Black workers as strikebreakers. Incensed by this threat to their status, White workers responded by employing "exclusionary" and/or "caste" strategies. Namely, White workers attempted to exclude Blacks entirely from the workforce or relegate Black labor to the least desirable jobs. In this formulation, White workers are seen as a primary force in the marginalization of Blacks to inferior jobs.

Since the 1980s, the dominant labor history approach to workplace race relations has taken its cue from Bonacich and the vitriolic "Gutman (and his supporters) vs. Hill" debates (among others, see Brier 1989; Gutman 1968; Hill 1987, 1988, 1996, 2002; Lichtenstein 1995). A new wave of scholarship has focused on the role of White workers' racism in marginalizing Black workers. Special attention has been given to the role of White-run unions' attitudes and policies toward non-White workers. Among labor historians, it is now widely accepted that White workers often sought to maintain a racialized workplace hierarchy—for example, in the iron and steel industry (Nelson 2001), coal mining (Letwin 1998), and meatpacking (Street 1996). These authors contend that White workers held clear conceptions about the appropriateness of particular jobs as "White man's work," delineated from the dirty and arduous "Black man's work." McKiven (2011) articulates this perspective succinctly: "the caste system, and the ideology of White supremacy that supported it, was essential to the defense of their (White workers) class interests" (4).

Considerable attention has also been paid to the relationship between unions and Black workers. Numerous scholars have highlighted the role of unions in maintaining Whites' access to privileged jobs and barring African American workers from occupational advancement (among others, see Draper 1994; Foner 1982; McKiven 2011; Nelson 2001; Tuttle 1970). Norrell (1986) argues that CIO unions (Congress of Industrial Unions) in the steel industry gave White workers "new power to enforce job discrimination, thus severely curtailing Black opportunities'' (670). Academic Herbert Hill, a former NAACP labor secretary, was the most vocal critic of CIO unions and White workers in general. Hill relies heavily on lawsuits filed by Black workers across various industries to support his contention that organized White labor often colluded with employers to keep Black workers from moving up the occupational hierarchy (Hill 1996, 1998, 2002).

Academics interested in the process of "White" racial formation among European immigrants have also significantly contributed to our understanding of race and work (Allen 1994; Brattain 2001; Ignatiev 1994; Jacobson 1999; Roediger 1999, 2005). Among other things, these authors have focused on the discourse European immigrants and their offspring utilized to conceptualize Black people as the "other." Roediger's *Wages of Whiteness* (1999) was inspired by Du Bois's ([1935]1993) argument that, as a result of racialized hierarchies, White workers received a "psychological wage" to compensate for capitalist exploitation.

> The White group of laborers, while they receive a low wage, were compensated in part by a sort of public and psychological wage. They were given public deference and titles of courtesy because they were White. They were admitted freely with all classes of White people to public functions, public parks, and the best schools. (DuBois [1935]1993, 700)

This argument posits that the "psychological wage" prevented White workers from viewing Black workers as equals and undermined the potential for interracial working-class solidarity. Roediger (1999) argues that because the "White" working class in the United States emerged within a slaveholding republic—they came to view themselves in opposition to what they were not: "Blacks" and enslaved people. Roediger (1999) and Ignatiev (1994) both focus heavily on the intense efforts of Irish immigrants to differentiate themselves from Black people and establish their place as "White" Americans deserving of all the privileges White skin afforded. Roediger (2005) argues that during the 1920s (marked by restrictive immigration laws), European ethnic groups became "White." These first- and second-generation European immigrants coalesced around labor struggles, racial structures at work, and the enforcement of racially restricted home ownership rules, which ensured all "White" neighborhoods. "White" race formation literature underscores the divisiveness that existed within the working class along racial lines and the extent to which becoming "White" meant distancing themselves from African Americans.

Sociological research provides us with useful conceptual frameworks for interpreting the strategies undertaken by White workers to gain occupational advantages over their non-White counterparts (Reskin 2000, 2003; Smith

2002; Tilly 1998; Tomaskovic-Devey 1993; Waldinger 1997; Weeden 2000). Research findings suggest that racial (and gender) hierarchies at work have remained remarkably stable across industries and periods. On the whole, women and non-Whites are more likely than White males to work in lower-status jobs and to receive lower wages in return for their labor. Recent literature on opportunity hoarding and social closure suggests that more privileged workers (White males) also participate in creating material inequality.

It has been demonstrated that White males engage in "opportunity hoarding" at work, a process whereby they actively attempt to exclude non-Whites and/or women from access to higher-status jobs (Tilly 1998). White males have also been found to engage in "social closure." This Weberian concept refers to the myriad of mechanisms (for example, refusing to train non-White male workers, pressuring employers to hire only friends or family members) used to maintain and create occupational barriers and economic advantages for White male workers. The consequence of "social closure" is often the reproduction of racial, ethnic, and gender inequality among workers (Tilly 1998; Tomaskovic-Devey and Skaggs 1999, 2002; Waldinger 1997; Weeden 2000). Strikingly, Waldinger (1997) argues that even low-skilled workers can attempt to engage in social closure and refuse to train new workers they do not like. Historical accounts provide compelling evidence that White workers often tried to exclude non-Whites from apprenticeships and on-the-job training (Arnesen 1994; Foner and Lewis 1981; Hill 1962, 1996, 2002; McKiven 1995; Minchin 2001; Nelson 2000; Street 1996).

In short, sociological perspectives (specifically, social closure and opportunity hoarding) and historical studies provide useful conceptual frameworks and ample evidence that White workers did indeed actively participate in relegating non-White workers to inferior jobs. However, regardless of how much power White labor possessed (relative to Black workers), one cannot assume that White workers had more power in determining Black people's low status at work than employers did. In fact, in all three cases, employers created race-gender hierarchies, exclusions, and segregation in the workforce before and in the absence of organized White male laborers making such demands.

In addition to the racial competition model, which focuses on White workers, there exists an abundant body of literature in economics and sociology that suggests that employers are essential actors in the production of racial inequality at work. The work reviewed next focuses on explanations for historical discrimination. (The final chapter of this book delves into the exemplary contemporary sociological literature on employers and race-gender inequality in the workplace.)

Employers Engage in Racial Discrimination

There is a vast amount of literature discussing employers and racial discrimination. Overall, these works indicate that employers play a significant role in creating and manipulating racial divisions. What follows is a review of some key concepts that inform this work.

Some academics have argued that discrimination against workers of color benefited employers because it provided them with a group to "super-exploit." Pettigrew (1985) outlines the key benefits employers accrue from the "super-exploitation" of Black workers. First, African Americans serve as a reserve labor force, providing flexibility to address fluctuations in business cycles. Second, Black Americans often find themselves compelled to undertake undesirable tasks out of desperation. Furthermore, their wealth is usually transferred to the White bourgeoisie, contributing to capitalists' capital accumulation. Last, Black workers contribute to stabilizing the system by creating divisions within the working class. From this perspective, employers are the financial beneficiaries of Black workers' marginalization within the occupational hierarchy. Countless cases have examined how employers benefit from racial discrimination against Afro-descended people because it provides them with a group of "super-exploited" workers. By deeming specific work "Black jobs," employers were able to pay lower wages, thereby extracting even greater profits (for examples, see Blauner 1972; DuBois [1935]1993; Foner 1982; Marks 1981; Nelson 2001; Trotter 1985, 1990).

The Pullman Company's employment of Black men and porters certainly fits with the "racialized super-exploitation" perspective. This perspective underscores the Pullman Company executives' efforts to garner greater profits as a central part of their practice of relegating Black men to the least desirable jobs on the train. However, this perspective does not shed light on why Pullman Company executives did not decide to employ African American men as conductors and super-exploit their labor in the conductor occupation. Neither can it explain why Black male workers were not utilized in the airline industry when they were less expensive than White female workers.

"Divide and Conquer"

W. E. B. Du Bois brilliantly provides some of the earliest argumentation that White aristocrats and employers accrued economic benefits from the creation of racialized work hierarchies in the United States. In Du Bois's classic work *White Reconstruction in America* ([1935]1993), he contends that southern elites fomented racial antagonism among poor Whites and Blacks to undermine any potential interracial class solidarity. Furthermore, he posits that this racial antipathy had been "carefully planned" and that "southern capital accepted race hate and Black disenfranchisement as a permanent program of exploitation." Indeed, Southern capital had created a "policy of divide-and-rule" through which "well-to-do planters and the southern ruling class generally . . . derived a benefit from the struggle that White and Black workers were carrying on between themselves" ([1935]1993, 630). Du Bois argued that racial antagonism and Black workers' oppression were directly attributable to the actions of capital.

The underlying premise of the "divide and conquer" framework is that employers would face serious economic costs via higher wages, better working conditions, and worker benefits if they were confronted by a unified working class. To prevent an interracial working class from seriously challenging the economic order, employers created racialized work hierarchies, separate mobility ladders, and, when necessary, fomented and manipulated racial antagonism among workers. Roemer's (1979) work on the micro-foundations of a Marxian (divide and conquer) theory of racial wage discrimination reaches a similar conclusion.

Roemer (1979, 703) argues that when Black and White workers are "mixed in certain proportions, racial discord is introduced in their ranks." Racial discord arises because of the broader racism in society. As a result of this racial disharmony, working-class solidarity is undermined, thereby reducing the bargaining power of both Black and White workers and allowing capital to lower the wages of both groups.

Another mechanism described to divide the working class is "labor market segmentation." Michael Piore (1972, 2) summarizes this perspective succinctly:

> The primary hypothesis of the dual labor market was that the labor market is divided into two essentially *distinct* sectors, termed the *primary* and the *secondary* sectors. The former offers jobs with relatively high wages, good working conditions, chances of advancement, equity, and due process in the administration of work rules, and, above all, employment stability. Jobs in the secondary sector, by contrast, tend to be low paying, with poorer working conditions, little chance of advancement; a highly personalized relationship between workers and supervisors which leaves wide latitude for favoritism and is conducive to harsh and capricious work discipline; and with considerable instability in jobs and a high turnover among the labor force.

Piore (1972) argues that historical decisions made primarily by employers have arbitrarily assigned different kinds of work (which could be performed in either sector) to the secondary or primary sector. Furthermore, discrimination perpetuates labor market segmentation by restricting Black workers to secondary sector jobs.

"A Theory of Labor Market Segmentation" by Reich, Gordon, and Edwards (1973) provides an economic-historical account of labor market segmentation. The authors argue that labor market segmentation originated during the transition from competitive to monopoly capitalism in 1890. During the competitive era of capitalism (before 1890), developments in the labor market pointed toward the homogenization, not segmentation, of workers. Increasing mechanization created standardized work requirements, and large factories brought large numbers of workers into a shared environment of toil. The increasingly homogenized and proletarian nature of the workforce engendered tensions, which were revealed by a "tremendous upsurge in labor conflict that accompanied the emergence of monopoly capitalism" (Reich, Gordon, and Edwards 1973, 360).

Accompanying the homogenization of the workforce was the emergence of "oligopolistic corporations," which began consolidating their power. These large corporations were released from the pressures of short-run competition and were free to pursue long-term strategies for labor control. Reich, Gordon, and Edwards (1973, 361) argue:

> The new needs of monopoly capitalism for control were threatened by the consequences of homogenization and proletarianization of the workforce. Evidence abounds that corporations were painfully aware of the potentially revolutionary character of these movements . . .The employers' mass offensive on unions between 1903 and 1908 was more of an ideological crusade than a matter of specific demands. . . . The historical analysis suggests that to meet this threat, employers actively and consciously fostered labor market segmentation in order to 'divide and conquer' the labor force. . . . The central thrust of the new strategies was to break down the increasingly unified worker interests that grew out of the proletarianization of work and the concentration of workers in urban areas. As exhibited in several aspects of these large firms' operations, this effort aimed to divide the labor force into various segments so that the actual experiences of workers were different and the basis of their common opposition to capitalists undermined.

This segmentation process included the creation of "internal labor markets" (job ladders and tiers) and the erection of barriers between primary and secondary jobs. Reich, Gordon, and Edwards (1973) also argue that employers consciously exploited racial and ethnic antagonism to undercut unionism and break strikes. Their account suggests that employers are primarily to blame for the creation of dual labor markets and, therefore, also responsible for the placement of African Americans within the secondary (inferior) labor market sector. To prevent a unified working class from seriously challenging the economic order, employers created racialized work hierarchies, separate mobility ladders, and, when necessary, fomented/manipulated racial antagonism among workers.

Challenging and Refining "Divide and Conquer" Theory

Evidence suggests that in some cases, employers did bring in Black workers with the intention of undermining White workers' aspirations—this is commonly referred to as part of a "divide and conquer" strategy. Bonacich (1976, 1979) provides the most compelling and persuasive argument against the "divide and conquer" theory concerning Black and White workers. Bonacich argues against neo-Marxist theories, which believe they can explain why a social fact (namely racial discrimination) exists simply by claiming that it benefits capitalists. Such "Marxist functionalism" is flawed because it is "based on the reasoning that the end-state determines the processes which lead to it" (1979, 39).

Bonacich's version of racial split labor market theory presumes that employers maintain a laissez-faire attitude toward racial divisions and conflict among workers. In Bonacich's view, capitalists' principal motivation is to hire the cheapest labor available, regardless of race. Split labor market theory posits that capital supports a liberal or laissez-faire ideology that would permit all workers to compete freely in an open market. Such competition would displace higher-paid labor. "Only under duress does business yield to a labor aristocracy" (Bonacich 1972, 557).

Bonacich argues that employers lack economic incentives to maintain a racial caste system at work. Her theoretical stance regarding employers' role is summarized as:

> If employers create a price differential, they must be paying one group of workers more than they have to, which would only be rational if paying more to one group enabled them to pay another substantially less. Capital would have to be "bribing" White labor to help keep Black labor cheap. Such a convoluted strategy may indeed be in operation, but a number of facts argue against it. First, as we have seen, workers do not enter the labor market with a clean slate upon which the employer arbitrarily marks his price; there are forces that differentiate the labor force before he touches it. Second, a strategy of bribery is hard to combine with the facts of displacement and strikebreaking. If capital wanted to keep White labor loyal, why undermine them? (1976, 44)

Conceptually, employers are depicted as operating solely based on rational economic motivations:

> (The) capitalist class [are] faced with (rather than creating) a labor market differentiated in terms of bargaining power (or price). Capital turns toward the cheaper labor pool as a more desirable workforce, a choice consistent with the simple pursuit of higher profits. Higher priced labor resists being displaced,

> and the racist structures they erect to protect themselves are antagonistic to the interests of capital. (Bonacich 1976, 44)

In this formulation, racial divisions and hierarchies result from the actions of White workers attempting to exclude and remain more powerful than workers of color. White workers' efforts to exclude non-White workers from the labor market failed. Instead, by the 1930s, White labor created a caste system dividing "Black work" from "White work," thus excluding Black labor from certain jobs.

Contrary to Bonacich's "split labor market theory," the "divide and conquer" theory posits that employers played an active role in creating racial hierarchies within the workforce and that they did so to control the working class and maximize profits. These competing perspectives—employers were merely responding to White workers' racist, exclusionary, and/or caste strategies, or employers actively participated in manipulating racial antagonism and creating racialized hierarchies—are seemingly difficult to reconcile—however, the scholarship on racialized paternalism attempts to address these seeming contradictions.

Racialized Paternalism

Historical sociologists have demonstrated the importance of racialized paternalism in conceptualizing employers' behavior. Boswell, Brown, Bruegemann, and Peters (2006) discuss employers' role in maintaining working-class divisions by focusing on paternalism. They argue that the role of employer paternalism has not been integrated into split labor market theory. The authors contend that this lack of emphasis on paternalistic relations between capital and one race of workers has obscured employers' active role in dividing the working class.

Racialized paternalism occurs when employers offer one group of workers services such as housing, the extension of credit/loans, and sponsorship of local social institutions. Paternalism is profitable for the employer because the "services" they offer workers are contingent upon worker loyalty and docility. "(Paternalism) raises the costs of labor conflict for workers, including quitting, which increases the power of managers or employers to exploit workers" (Boswell et al. 2006, 29). When employer paternalism is racialized, "one racial group is 'bought off' by capital. Economic rewards and other privileges prevent this segment from engaging in class struggle and represent another means of instilling working-class divisions" (Boswell et al., 2006, 26). Racialized paternalism, the authors contend, explains how employers' discrimination along racial lines can be both rational and profitable.

Pullman indeed engaged in "majority paternalism" regarding his White workers—they were given privileges (conductor jobs, company town housing, reasonable pensions) that Black workers were denied. One could also contend that by providing Black men with a job monopoly on the trains, Pullman was also engaging in "minority paternalism." Similarly, airline executives engaged in a form of "race-gender paternalism" in their treatment of White female flight attendants. It can be argued that employers in all three cases enacted a version of the "divide and conquer" approach to the workforce. In the railroad and airline industries, "race-gender paternalism" was used to segregate (porters from conductors and pilots from flight attendants) as a means of obviating any unified labor demands from all workers. In the case of cruise ships, employers actively recruit a multinational labor force to divide crew members.

Racialized Systems of Inequality

Several perspectives exist for comprehending the influence of race in determining societal consequences. Race is a fundamental dimension of social structure in the United States. "Racial formation" refers to the sociohistorical phenomenon in which racial categories are established, occupied, altered, and ultimately dismantled (Omi and Winant 2014). This perspective asserts that the belief in "race" is not a timeless idea. Instead, it is perceived as a societal construct influenced by historical circumstances, characterized by its lack of stability and fixed nature, and subject to ongoing political debates and disputes. Race is an essential component of social structure at both the individual and societal levels. The concept of "racial projects" refers to the deliberate actions taken by different individuals and groups within a community to either perpetuate or contest racial inequalities across numerous aspects of social existence.

The United States may be seen as a racist social system in which many aspects, such as the economy, politics, society, and ideology, are influenced to some extent by the categorization of individuals into racial groups (Bonilla-Silva 1997; Glenn 2002). The process of racialization within a given culture invariably involves the establishment of racial hierarchies, wherein a particular race is attributed with superior characteristics and subsequently benefits from social, political, psychological, and economic advantages, while other groups are assigned an inferior position. Consequently, racism does not exist as an autonomous intellectual framework or emerge from individual "irrationality." Racism is posited to have a structural basis. Once a society has been racialized, race-based structures come into existence, and these socially constructed "races" develop divergent objective interests.

> After the process of attaching meaning to a "people" is instituted, race becomes a real category of group association and identity social relations between the races become institutionalized (forming a structure as well as a culture) and affect their social life whether individual members of the races want it or not. (Bonilla-Silva 1997, 472–3)

Because the races are afforded unequal treatment at all levels of society, they develop divergent group interests. Therefore, these racial interests are collective, not individual, in nature. In other words, Whites as a group had a shared interest in maintaining the social structure that afforded them benefits as the privileged race.

From this perspective, White executives had both a financial and structural motive (as Whites) to create and maintain a racial hierarchy in the transportation service sector. For example, the company's century-long practice of putting White men in charge of Black workers on the train was a result of White men's (company executives) desire to maintain and reinforce the larger structure of racialized inequality. Therefore, employers' discrimination against African Americans is entirely rational given the racial interests of employers as White Americans.

Gendered Systems of Inequality

Similar argumentation has arisen around gender inequality. Scholars have moved away from biologically defined understandings of sex differences. Sociologists and feminist historians have utilized gender as an analytical concept that refers to the myriad of ways in which social relationships, identities, and socially constructed meanings are assigned to reproductive differences (Scott 1986; Laslett and Brenner 1989). "The core of the definition (gender) rests on an integral connection between two propositions; gender is a constitutive element of social relationships based on perceived differences between the sexes, and gender is a primary way of signifying relationships of power" (Scott 1986, 1067). Another perspective on gender moves beyond focusing on reproductive differences. These scholars assert that gender is an organizing principle in all social institutions (Acker 1990).

Historians of gender have more often articulated the importance of both material interests and ideology in shaping gender inequality (Glenn 2002; Hartman 1981). Scholars have also explored the role of both male workers and employers in marginalizing, excluding, and devaluing women's labor (Kessler-Harris 1990; Witz 1990). The marginalization of women to less desirable jobs, it has been argued, was the result of male workers' efforts to maintain gender privilege. By the 1890s, business owners systematically sought to maximize profits by undercutting the position of skilled White male laborers. One such tactic included "deskilling"—breaking down the production processes into smaller jobs that cheaper unskilled, semi-skilled laborers could perform. Mechanization allowed employers to replace White male skilled workers with women. In response to this threat, native-born White men and their unions utilized a variety of tactics to exclude women from trade occupations (Kessler-Harris 1982).

Scholars have also argued that White male workers relied upon ideologies of "White manhood" and the "cult of true womanhood" to justify pushing women, especially White women, out of the labor force to maintain both their material interests and their culturally ascribed dominant position in the home and family (Hartman 1976). Just as White workers are seen as an essential factor in the marginalization of non-Whites, it is argued that male workers played a significant role in the exclusion and/or marginalization of female workers.

Intersectionality

Intersectionality is one of the most significant contributions to social science. Unfortunately, although the term is frequently used, its origins are often neglected.

Sojourner Truth's *Ain't I a Woman* is understood to be one of the first articulations of the paradigm that race, gender, and class must be understood as inexplicably linked together. As documented in countless works, subsequent generations of Black feminist organizations, activists, and scholars such as Angela Davis, Patricia Hill Collins, and The Combahee River Collective, to name just a few, would continue to deepen this perspective in theory and praxis.

The term "intersectionality" was introduced to scholarly circles by Kimberlé Crenshaw, a critical race theorist and legal scholar. Crenshaw coined the term to describe the simultaneous and interconnected forms of discrimination experienced by Black women. She specifically highlighted the limitations of prevailing approaches in antidiscrimination law, feminist theory, and anti-racist activism that primarily center on the experiences of the most advantaged individuals within marginalized groups. Crenshaw specifically emphasized legal examples in which women were compelled to decide between pursuing a claim of racial discrimination or gender discrimination without the ability to assert that they had experienced discrimination as a result of the intersection of both race and gender.

Utilizing the intersectional perspective, numerous works on race and labor have repeatedly demonstrated that race, ethnicity, class, and gender should be studied in conjunction with each other to best understand the various dimensions of inequality experienced by different groups (among many others, see Ammott and Matthaei 1991; Browne and Misra 2003; Collins 2022; Glenn 2002).

Whiteness as Management

There is a deep-rooted connection between institutionalized racism and labor management in the United States. "Whiteness as management" was created and honed from 1830 to 1930. This concept refers to the labor management philosophy adopted by White employers and specialists, which was developed within the context of ongoing White-racist discourse and action. The coevolution of the "scientific" management of employees and the White-racist framing of society occurred during this era, as well as in the ensuing decades that followed. During the period spanning from 1830 to 1930, a significant portion of White discourse and efforts about labor management revolved around strategies for overseeing individuals of African descent who were enslaved. During subsequent decades, there was a shift in attention toward Southern and Eastern European immigrant workers and employees from other racial backgrounds. Across various contexts, such as plantations, mines, timber, railroad construction, and meatpacking plants, innovative managerial strategies were consistently utilized to exploit the variations among individuals and employees. These techniques were documented in management journals, refined, and widely shared among elite White men. To be clear, labor was not an "abstract" concept. Managers played a significant role in generating and exploiting social disparities among individuals based on factors such as race, ethnicity, nationality, religion, geography, and gender (Esch 2018; Roediger and Esch 2009, 2012).

"Whiteness as management" is a framework that applies to all three cases examined in this book. It allows us to understand how capitalists' racialization of workers was central to the development of employment relations in the railroad, airline, and cruise industries.

Last, the framework developed in this book draws heavily upon W. E. B Du Bois's argumentation in his lesser-read works Souls of White Folks and Hands of Ethiopia, where he brilliantly demonstrates that Europeans' colonization of the Americas, Africa, and Asia was both a materialist *and* ideological project. Specifically, Du Bois contends that colonization was undoubtedly an economic enterprise geared toward extraction and exploitation. Simultaneously, it was a project designed to spread:

> This theory of human culture and its aims has worked itself through warp and woof of our daily thought with a thoroughness that few realize. Everything great, good, efficient, fair, and honorable is "white"; everything mean, bad, blundering, cheating, and dishonorable is "yellow"; a bad taste is "brown"; and the devil is "black. The changes of this theme are continually rung in picture and story, in newspaper heading and moving-picture, in sermon and school book, until, of course, the King can do no wrong,—a White Man is always right and a Black Man has no rights which a white man is bound to respect." (DuBois 1969, 22)

Drawing upon the various theoretical frameworks previously discussed, this work conceptualizes employers' actions utilizing a structural (as opposed to individual psychology) explanation. This conceptual framework views employers as being driven by both (1) profit motives to exploit racialized-gendered "cheap labor" and (2) their own racial-gender prejudices and interests as members of the dominant racial-gender group.

The literature on employers discussed in this chapter clarifies that employers play some role in creating and reproducing racial inequality at work. Employers were responding to or manipulating prevailing racial ideology, and they also played a significant role in forming these racialized structures to begin with. Racial ideology does not simply come into play when there is actual or potential labor contestation; instead, the very understanding of who is appropriate for specific jobs is inextricably linked to creating those job categories to begin with. In this sense, White workers (and privileged workers in general) engage in discriminatory behavior against marginalized workers and attempt to hoard good jobs for themselves. However, they are doing this based on racial ideology and practices that were initially established by White elites. Therefore, it is imperative to understand the circumstances and decisions made when employers originally created job categories. The following chapters examine the origins of the porter, flight attendant, and service crew member jobs. Special attention will be paid to what employers themselves said about the race-gender typing of these occupations.

Data and Methods

When the Pullman Company ceased operations, it donated its company records to the Newberry Library in Chicago, Illinois. I made numerous trips to the archives to gather data. Using a digital camera to capture images, I collected significant amounts of data for later scrutiny. Specifically, I analyzed the following data in the Pullman Company archives: internal correspondence among executives, hiring memoranda, employee instruction manuals, personnel records, employment applications, training evaluations, disciplinary files, discharge records, and the company newsletter. This archive provides an opportunity to analyze both employers' stated intentions and actual outcomes regarding race and gender inequality on Pullman trains. For the airline and cruise industry data, I relied heavily on existing scholarship and, when possible, analyzed the available primary data, focusing on employers' stated reasons for hiring certain workers, training manuals, and industry reports.

Analytical Strategy

I systematically examined company archives (and secondary literature), seeking any evidence that was directly or indirectly related to the creation or enforcement of a race-gender division of labor and the reasons for that division. An indication of the sort of evidence that would suggest employers' racial ideology shaped workplace hierarchies:

(A) Statements by executives that only certain sorts of workers are appropriate for specific jobs in ways that explicitly or indirectly conform to existing race-gender lines.
(B) Actions or statements by executives aimed at maintaining/reinforcing existing race-gender segmentation, unless this is done as a response to demands by White and/or male workers.
(C) Statements or evidence by management that reveal their race-gender attitudes and ideologies in ways that plausibly seem likely to influence employment decisions, even if those attitudes are not explicitly connected to immediate employment decisions.

Outline of the Book

Chapter 2 examines the origins of the Pullman Company, beginning in 1858 and ending in the 1880s. The central question for this chapter is how the porter job came to be held by Black men and only by Black men, and the conductor job came to be held by White men and only by White men. The crucial consideration appears to have been decisions made by George Pullman that were apparently driven by economic concerns. The role of George Pullman's racial ideology is challenging to discern because no first-hand accounts exist regarding this issue. What is clear, however, is that from the very beginning, the conductor and porter jobs were structured in ways that explicitly reflected a racial hierarchy. It was in this era that the system of racialized paternalism was created.

Chapter 3 focuses explicitly on Pullman Company executives' public and private racial discourse from the 1890s to the 1950s. This chapter examines how the job requirements for porters and conductors reproduced a hierarchy of masculinity in and outside of the workplace. Special attention is paid to the relationship between the construction of Black versus White masculinity. Porters worked as servants on the trains. They received meager wages, relied on tips, and were expected to constantly remain on call, shine shoes, babysit White children, serve food, make up beds, clean up after others, and do it all with a perpetual smile. Conductors, exclusively White men, were hired to oversee the porter and ensure that the Black man was appropriately performing his servility. By 1920, the Pullman Company was the largest single employer of Black men in the United States. The image of the safe, servile Pullman porter was ubiquitous in popular culture, appearing as caricatures in newspapers, magazines, songs, radio, television, and films. Some topics covered in this chapter include feminizing the Black male worker, constructing Black masculinity as a caretaker of White womanhood and children, and naturalizing Black male servility.

Chapter 4 explores the origins of race-gender segregation in the airline industry. During the first wave (the 1910s to 1930s) of piloting, women challenged prevailing gender norms and took to the skies. However, once airline companies became institutionalized, employers would banish all women and people of color from the cockpit until the 1970s, thereby cementing the link between White masculinity and piloting. The flight attendant is an occupation created in 1930. Once employers decided to hire White women to serve airline passengers, the nature of the job itself would be transformed. In this new job, employers would structure work in ways that reproduced the dynamics of White heteropatriarchy, with flight attendants, passengers, and pilots all performing within these confines. Once the job was deemed White women's work, the bodies of flight attendants would be widely marketed. This chapter traces how flight attendants are depicted as the all-American girl next door in the 1940s to 1960s but shift to overt hypersexualization by the late 1960s. This emphasis on the appearance of flight attendants was explicit in the hiring process, and regulations of women's appearance were rigidly enforced before each flight. Employers systematically excluded Black women from the job. They spent a great deal of money and effort to resist integrating their workforce until compelled to do so, following multiple lawsuits and pressure campaigns.

Chapter 5 examines employers' creation of workplace hierarchies in the modern U.S.-based cruise ship industry. A typical cruise ship leaving from a port in the United States contains workers from seventy-five to ninety nationalities. Due to the "flags of convenience" system, cruise ship owners are immune from meaningful labor laws banning discrimination along racial, ethnic, or national lines. In this instance, employers are essentially left to their own devices when creating and maintaining unequal employment conditions for their employees. The dividing lines between employees are the officer, staff, and crew designations, which occur primarily based on the worker's nationality. Officers and staff members are predominantly from the Global North. Crew members are almost exclusively from the Global South. These workers are paid meager wages, work ten to fourteen hours daily, live below the decks, and are away from home for at least six months. In this case, Eastern Europeans occupy an in-between role whereby they are more likely to be given the more desirable job opportunities among crew members. Although cruise ships are genuinely international workplaces, Filipino men are overrepresented in the ranks of frontline service workers. This chapter concludes with the racialized discourse deployed to explain why Filipino men are "best suited" for service work.

The conclusion summarizes the key findings of the book. It moves the narrative to the present day by examining the sociological work that addresses the ongoing issues around race, gender, and ethnic hierarchies in the workforce. Unlike the periods and contexts previously discussed, it is currently unlawful for employers to discriminate against workers based on race, gender, or ethnicity. However, even in the post–civil rights era, an abundance of excellent scholarship demonstrates that employers continue to play a role in reproducing various types of inequality in the labor market.

Chapter 2

The Origins of Service Workers in the Pullman Railroad Company, 1858–1880s

This chapter examines the origins of the Pullman Company, beginning in 1858 and ending in the 1880s. A significant challenge for this chapter is the relative sparsity of company data (compared to later periods). It is not unexpected that the types of bureaucratic data that are available from the 1890s (e.g., personnel records, disciplinary codes) did not exist in prior decades. Additionally, in 1871, a fire destroyed some company files related to its initial operations. However, regardless of the challenges, examining this period is critical to understanding initial hiring practices and how jobs were originally structured. The central question for this chapter is how the porter job came to be held by Black men and only by Black men, and the conductor job came to be held by White men and only by White men. The crucial consideration appears to have been decisions made by George Pullman, apparently driven by economic considerations. The role of George Pullman's racial ideology is hard to discern because no first-hand accounts exist regarding this issue. What is clear, however, is that from the very beginning, the conductor and porter jobs were structured in ways that explicitly reflected a racial hierarchy.

The chapter begins by briefly reviewing relevant literature, then discusses the Pullman Company's early history before focusing on the character of the porter and conductor jobs and alternative explanations as to why employers assigned the porter job exclusively to Black men. The chapter concludes with an analysis of exactly how the company racialized positions on the train, a comparison of company policy as it pertained to White and Black workers, and a discussion of the findings.

In light of the current disadvantages that Black male workers face in the service sector, it is especially crucial to understand the role of the Pullman porter. Black men's first mass entrance into wage labor was as the ultimate servant for the traveling public. Analyzing why and how this conceptualization of Black men's labor was created, marketed, and exploited deepens our understanding of the socially constructed nature of both race and gender norms, ideologies, and practices. The idea that Black men are "naturally suited" to be servants who can even be trusted to take care of White women and babies is an anathema today. The Pullman Porter case exemplifies how the content of racialization is immensely flexible and can be deployed by those in power in a myriad of ways.

In examining the causes of race-gender inequality, it is especially useful to focus on processes at the organizational level. An ideal-typic case study allows us to fully conceptualize why, when, and how these hierarchies were created, reinforced, and challenged. Organizations are vital sites where racial and gender inequality is created and reproduced. There is consensus in the organization literature that inertia, the fact that organizations tend to be resistant to change over time, is a factor in shaping social outcomes within businesses. Once organizational practices and structures are established, they become hard to change (Stinchcombe 1965). Furthermore, Stainback, Tomaskovic-Devey, and Skaggs (2010) identify inertia as "probably the most powerful force affecting workplace inequality and tends to reproduce organizational divisions of labor, the demographic composition of jobs, and the relative power, status, compensation, and respect afforded different actors over time" (2). For these reasons, it is particularly important to understand the emergence of racialized workplace hierarchies on Pullman trains.

Organizations are also one key arena "in which widely disseminated cultural images of gender are invented and reproduced" (Acker 1990, 140). Employers play a role in spreading cultural images regarding race, and organizations also invent and reproduce racial hierarchies. Focusing on a specific case allows for an in-depth analysis of company policies over the years. The motivations and consequences of these policies are essential to understand in light of the persistent racial-gender inequality in the U.S. labor market. Contemporarily, a host of racial-ethnic-gender-class ideologies are used to justify why certain groups of workers are overrepresented and underrepresented in various occupations. Understanding how these contemporary ideological justifications for workplace inequality draw upon and diverge from historical ideologies is integral to interpreting current company policies that intentionally or unintentionally reproduce race-ethnic-gender hierarchies.

One explanation would assume that it was only rational and inevitable that Pullman would create a new job (porter) exclusively for Black men. Black men were cheap "super-exploitable" (Pettigrew 1985) laborers and happy to have a job outside of the oppressive South. But this simple explanation does not leave room to consider: Why not White men? Why not Black women? Why not White women? Why not hire any worker capable of doing the porter job? That an occupational category was created by Pullman exclusively for

Black men and remained that way for over one hundred years merits an examination of why that was the case. The only exception to this practice occurred in 1925, when, in response to the establishment of the first union representing porters, the company hired some Filipino men to work as club car attendants (Posadas 1982). Other than that brief moment, for over 100 years, the role of the Pullman porter was inextricably tied to Black masculinity.

It is essential to remember that employers are not only operating within and adhering to the context of proscribed social norms, but that in this instance, the employer played a significant role in constructing and marketing to the public a view of Black manhood that normalized and legitimized their servitude. Also, to garner a more nuanced understanding of race-gender inequality in U.S. labor history, it is important to understand the role of racial ideology in racializing the porter job as "Black man's work" for several reasons. The racialization of Black men's labor was even more complicated than one might originally imagine. It should be a well-known social fact that

> southern White conceptions of Black men centered in their supposed animalistic nature, emotionality, lack of higher intelligence, and unrestrained sexuality. Lazy and prone to crime, they required a strong, controlling White hand. Contradictorily, they were depicted as either shiftless and slow-witted buffoons or dangerous rapists. (Glenn 2002, 254)

Most notably, in 1915, this degrading portrayal of Black masculinity as hypersexual and violence-prone was disseminated throughout the entire country in the wildly popular and influential film *Birth of Nation.*

Contrarily, the Pullman porter challenged these racial depictions and represented a parallel but divergent view of Black men that was advertised and disseminated nationwide. By 1920, Pullman was the country's single largest employer of Black men. Countering many existing archetypes, the image of the safe, servile Pullman porter was ubiquitous in the United States' popular culture, appearing as caricatures in newspapers, magazines, songs, and later on radio and television (Tye 2004). In this sense, the porter job was an important force in perpetuating this view of Black manhood across the nation. Outside of the South, the porter job helped shape White Americans' understanding of African American men.

A key aspect of understanding race-gender inequality is examining the rules of relationality expected in social interactions (Glenn 2002). In this instance, the dynamic explored is that between Black and White men on the trains. For this purpose, the nature of the conductor's job merits scrutiny. Similar to the strict company policy that porters be Black, the company also maintained for over a hundred years that only White men could be charged with the responsibility for overseeing the other workers on the train and collecting tickets. Analyzing how management attempted to regulate the relationship between conductors and porters can illuminate the role of employers' racial ideology in creating racialized workplace hierarchies.

COMPANY BACKGROUND

In 1855, Chicago was the fastest-growing city in the country. Having begun as a trading post, it was officially incorporated in 1833. Given its location on Lake Michigan, Chicago was a key location in the transportation of goods from east to west. Business people in the areas were also busy establishing large industries and financial institutions to support capitalist ventures. However, proximity to Lake Michigan was both a blessing and a curse. In the early years, constant flooding plagued the city, making it difficult to keep roads paved and businesses running smoothly. Although landowners balked at the costs, by 1855, the city government had decided the only solution was to raise the structures and roads along Lake Michigan and the Chicago River. George Pullman arrived in town to take advantage of the numerous contracts being handed out in the city of Chicago. George Pullman was successful in garnering lucrative contracts to raise buildings, and by 1858, he had accumulated $20,000 in wealth at the age of twenty-seven (Husband 1917).

Chicago was growing, and so was the railroad industry. In the mid-nineteenth century, railroad track construction exploded. The majority of this new construction took place in the Midwest in order to better connect it with the East Coast. For example, between 1850 and 1860, railroad track mileage tripled from 10,000 to 30,000 miles. With the incorporation of the western frontier, the writing was on the wall that eventually, the United States would need a transcontinental railroad to move people and goods across the country more efficiently.

Railroads were faster than other means of transportation, but the journey was still grueling. Railway cars were a bumpy ride, to say the least. The seats on these trains were narrow, with wooden backs and no cushioning. Passengers dealt with both sweltering heat in the summer and freezing temperatures in the winter. Trains had to make frequent stops so that passengers could get off the train and purchase what has been described as disgusting food at the train station. Also, because ownership and operation of railroad cars were splintered across various companies, passengers did not have access to direct long-distance travel from point A to point B.

When the terminal point of a trip was reached, the passenger disembarked and collected their baggage. The passenger then had to take their luggage and move on to another train station to get a train on a different railroad line. Because of the roundabout route passengers had to take, a trip from

Chicago to New York would cover 1,300 miles, 714 miles more than the straight distance. This lack of standardization extended to the tracks and railcars, which differed in width from one company to the next (Buder 1967; Husband 1917).

Pullman's First Sleeping Cars

Pullman was not the first to come up with the idea of making rail travel more comfortable. There were several other businessmen and companies engaged in the construction of sleeping cars. Notably, in 1858, the Wagner Sleeping Car Company and Woodruff Sleeping Car Company both manufactured sleeping cars that were in use on the railroads. George Pullman was just one of several capitalists who designed and converted old railcars into sleeping cars. He had garnered a contract with the Chicago and Alton Railroad company to convert two passenger cars into sleepers. Between 1858 and 1860, Pullman-designed cars were running between Chicago and other stops in the Midwest. Then the civil war began. The Union Army took over the operation of the Pullman cars to move troops (Husband 1917).

George Pullman went to the gold fields of Colorado and did not return to the sleeping car business until 1864. With $20,000 in hand, he set up shop in Chicago. He bought a plant, the necessary materials, and hired carpenters and mechanics to build what would become the most luxurious sleeping car to date. The "Pioneer" sleeping car was deemed a

> "wonder of the age. Brocaded fabrics covered the seats, and the door frames and window sashes were of hand-worked and polished wood. There was a plush red carpet, and several gilt-edged mirrors reflected the light of silver-trimmed coal oil lamps. During the day, the hinged upper berths (beds),cleverly concealed behind ornamented wood paneling were used to store bedding,which, consistent with the car's luxury, was of the finest quality" (Buder 1967, 10).

The "Pioneer" was a foot wider and two and a half feet higher than other cars in service. Pullman had built the impressive sleeping car prior to even obtaining a contract for its use by any railroad company. To operate the "Pioneer" railroad companies would be forced to narrow platforms and raise bridges to accommodate the girth of the new sleeping car. Unfortunately for George Pullman, none of the railroad companies were willing to do so. If not for the assassination of President Lincoln in 1865, George Pullman might never have operated a single railroad car, much less built a leading national company and achieved national notoriety (Buder 1967; Husband 1917).

For months, the "Pioneer" had gone unused, and George Pullman was unable to convince any railroad companies to pay the high cost to operate the sleeping car. After Lincoln was killed, a massive funeral procession was arranged from Washington to Springfield, Illinois, with all the pomp and ceremony befitting a martyred president. The Republican Party State Central Committee, headed by James H. Bowen, the president of the Third National Bank of Chicago, was responsible for planning the funeral procession from Chicago to Springfield. The committee selected the locally owned "Pioneer" to transport the president's casket and his wife. Right away, the state began raising bridges and narrowing platforms to accommodate the one-of-a-kind sleeping car. During the several-day trip to Springfield, the "Pioneer" garnered tremendous amounts of nationwide publicity and helped catapult George Pullman into the national limelight as an ingenious car builder. The job of selling railroad companies on his luxurious sleeping cars was made easier overnight (Buder 1967; Husband 1917).

George Pullman was not simply in the business of manufacturing sleeping cars. His intended business model involved maintaining ownership of the sleepers and control over their operations. Pullman's company would receive all the extra revenue from sleeping car fares, and the railroad company would receive all the proceeds from the passengers' regular fares while not having to pay for operation costs. This model was only profitable for railroad companies if the Pullman-brand sleeping car was able to generate increased passenger traffic. Impressed by all the national publicity Pullman garnered from Lincoln's funeral procession, the Chicago and Alton Railroad company signed a contract with George Pullman to carry the "Pioneer" on its lines. On May 25, 1865, the "Pioneer" sleeping car made its maiden voyage out of Chicago to St. Louis (Buder 1967; Husband 1917).

To generate even more public acclaim for his luxurious sleeping car, when not in operation, the "Pioneer" was part of exhibits targeting prominent civic groups and wealthy businessmen throughout the Midwest. George Pullman provided free passes to journalists and prominent citizens with the expectation that they would provide rave reviews for his impressive sleeping car. Creating a brand that was equated with luxury was incredibly important if Pullman was to convince passengers to pay the $2 surcharge the company charged (equal to more than a day's wage for an ordinary worker) and lure more railroad companies into signing contracts to carry Pullman sleeping cars. In August 1865, George Pullman negotiated a contract with the Michigan Central Railroad Company to carry another new Pullman sleeping car on their line between Chicago and Detroit. This was a lucrative contract for Pullman; due to passenger complaints, the Michigan Central Railroad Company replaced its own less-luxurious sleeping cars with one built by George Pullman's employees. The era of Pullman had begun.

In February 1867, the "Pullman's Palace Car Company" was granted a charter by the Illinois State Legislature. George Pullman had bought out his former business partners, the Field Brothers, and now maintained exclusive ownership over the sleeping car company. To raise additional capital to expand beyond the Midwest, Pullman offered an initial stock offering worth one million dollars, a tremendous sum in those days. These stocks were bought by local Chicago capitalists (Buder 1967). At the first meeting of the newly chartered Pullman Palace Car Company, George Pullman was elected to the board of directors (along with four others: H. E. Sargent, general superintendent of Michigan Central; Robert Harris, general superintendent of Chicago, Burlington, and Quincy; John Crerar, and Norman Williams Jr.). George Pullman was also elected the president and general manager of the company. He also retained controlling interests in the firm (Husband 1917).

Based on the success of the two sleeping cars already in operation, by the end of 1866, Pullman had built several other sleeping cars and had garnered numerous railroad companies willing to sign contracts with him. Forty-eight Pullman cars were in operation by the end of 1866, making Pullman the dominant sleeping car service in the Midwestern United States. Not content with dominating the Midwestern market, George Pullman moved his company into the Southern market. The southern railroad industry was devastated by the civil war and desperate to rebuild. In 1866, Pullman partnered with two other wealthy businessmen to form the Pullman, Kimball, and Ramsey Sleeping Car Company in Atlanta, Georgia. By 1868, ten major southern railroad companies had signed contracts with Pullman to use his sleeping cars. In 1870, Pullman bought out his partners and garnered complete control of the company, which was renamed the Pullman Southern Palace Car Company, which was under the central control of the Pullman Palace Car Company (Buder 1967; Husband 1917).

Pullman also came to dominate the sleeping car market in the Western United States. By 1869, the employees of the Central Pacific and Union Pacific railroad companies had completed building the transcontinental railroad. Trips to the West required a week of interrupted travel with few amenities along the way. The nation's desire to expand settler-colonialism to the West meant there would be plenty of passengers for the transcontinental trip from the East Coast. This was the perfect market for selling sleeping car services. Pullman was not the only capitalist eager to provide sleeping cars for the Western railroads. However, George Pullman gained exclusive contracts with the Western railroad companies by forging a mutually beneficial arrangement with a fellow capitalist, Andrew Carnegie. The two men formed a company called the Pullman Pacific Car Company in 1867 under the centralized control of the Pullman Palace Car Company. That same year, Pullman eventually acquired control of their main competitor for western sleepers, the Central Transportation Company. This acquisition brought with it entrée into the Eastern railroad market as well. Pullman's Company took over Central Transportation Company's contract with the Pennsylvania Railroad. That is, within five years, Pullman became a nationwide company (Buder 1967).

In 1870, Pullman decided to stop the practice of subcontracting construction of his sleepers out to various Midwestern yards. Pullman now wanted to manufacture his sleeping cars. He purchased a yard in Chicago and thus began the era of servicing and operating sleeping carsand building them. In the mid-1870s Pullman expanded his operation to build day coaches, dining cars, freight cars, and street cars (Hirsch 2003; Husband 1917). By 1881, the Pullman Palace Car Company earned an estimated $3 million and had over 800 cars operating across the United States and parts of Canada. By 1890, the company provided service for three-quarters of the railway mileage in the United States (Hirsh 2003). The company was profitable enough to consistently pay a quarterly dividend of at least 2 percent even through the economic downturns in the latter part of the century (Husband 1917).

Pullman's consistently profitable operation of sleeping cars highlights that the low wages paid to porters (discussed next) certainly was not the result of the porters' labor not generating sufficient income to merit higher wages.

The First Service Workers

When Pullman cars began running in 1858, workers on the train were all White men. Since most African Americans were still confined to slavery, it is unsurprising that Pullman did not employ Black men and women during these early years. The first Pullman passengers were greeted by a White conductor, Jonathan L. Barnes. In addition to "traditional" conductor tasks such as collecting tickets and assigning sleeping berths, White conductors performed the tasks that would later be assigned to a Black porter. These conductors were responsible for carrying passengers' luggage aboard, making beds, cleaning after passengers, and tending to their needs. Other young White men were also involved in tending to passengers' needs—some worked as waterboys who hawked ice-cold water and lemonade, and others sold snacks and newspapers throughout the train when it stopped at stations (Husband 1917).

Understanding why the White conductor was relieved of personal service responsibilities and replaced with the Black male porter is central to the issues of this book. Before directly tackling these issues, however, we need to understand what the porter job involved, which is essential information in considering who would be expected to perform servitude, and specifically why Black men held the job.

Starting in 1867, the Pullman Company employed only Black men as porters and in various other service occupations aboard the train. In addition to the sleeping car porter, there was the busboy, café/food service attendant, and private car porter. All of these employees were subject to the authority of the conductor. All these employees also had to learn how to operate and fix the trains' complex heating systems. Busboys were required to receive training in sleeping car porter service and food handling. They worked in buffets, café cars, and dining cars. They waited on passengers, set, and re-set tables. Café/food service attendants were trained in the same way that busboys were; additionally, they were taught to prepare the elaborate meals served on Pullman trains. Café/food service attendants were also expected to serve as sleeping car porters in train cars that contained both sleeping rooms and a buffet. Sleeping car porters also had many responsibilities in the yards and on board the train. While the cars were in the yards before a train run, porters were responsible for setting up the cars with linens, bedding, dining tables, and other necessities. Porters greeted passengers and got them settled into their sleeping quarters, which contained a bell that could summon a porter any time of day or night to fulfill a passenger's request. Porters made beds, cleaned up after passengers, shined everyone's shoes, mailed letters for passengers, and babysat young children while their parents traveled to the parlor cars to cavort, drink, play cards, and engage in other frivolities. Porters also cleaned and pressed clothing at the passengers' request, brought food to sleeping cars, and were expected to do all this with a permanent smile on their faces for days on end. It was not uncommon for porters to endure this harsh work for 400 hours a month (Perata 1996; Tye 2004). (See figures 2.1 and 2.2).

The Pullman Company executives replicated norms regarding Black-White interaction engendered by the racial hierarchy of the Jim Crow South in its railcars. Porters received very low wages and needed tips to supplement their earnings; by doing this, Pullman ensured that Black men were treated and acted like servants to support themselves. No other job within the Pullman Company necessitated workers relying on tips to survive. That Black men were not considered deserving of "White men's" wages necessary to support a family is highlighted by comparing the wages the company paid porters and the rent it charged in the company town. For example, in 1879, porters, on average, received $10 a month, while conductors earned $65 a month (Hirsch 2003, 10). Tellingly, the Pullman Company charged its White workers on average $14 a month for housing in the racially exclusionary company town (Buder 1967, 86), significantly more than porters' monthly wage of $10.

This disparity is even more glaring given the fact that the company scheduled work so that conductors had far more free time than porters. Unlike

Figure 2.1 Porters Serving Passengers in Railway Car 1882. *Source*: Schomburg Center for Research in Black Culture, Jean Blackwell Hutson Research and Reference Division, The New York Public Library. (1882). Passengers dining in a Pullman parlour railway car. Retrieved from https://digitalcollections.nypl.org/items/510d47df-b79e-a3d9-e040-e00a18064a99.

conductors, porters were not guaranteed even four hours of sleep a night. Porters were expected to be on call twenty-four hours a day, just in case a passenger rang their bell demanding some sort of personal service. Pullman built his trains so that conductors were ensured they would get a berth to sleep in at night by assigning conductors a designated sleeping place. Porters, on the other hand, only got a berth at the conductor's discretion if no passengers were in the same sleeping car. Otherwise, porters slept in the sitting room, where passengers drank, smoked, and played cars, or in part of the men's bathroom. Overall, the company created and structured the job in such a way that White men worked fewer hours yet were deemed worthy of much higher pay.

Employers attempting to maintain a system of surveillance over employees, was and remains, a key feature of the wage labor system for many workers; the Pullman Company was no different in this regard. Management went to great lengths to ensure that workers abided by the strict rules and hierarchy established on the train. The company frequently used "spotters" to spy on the workers aboard Pullman trains in order to ensure

Figure 2.2 Porters Working in the Pullman Car Kitchen. *Source*: Schomburg Center for Research in Black Culture, Jean Blackwell Hutson Research and Reference Division, The New York Public Library. (1882). Passengers dining in a Pullman parlour railway car. Retrieved from https://digitalcollections.nypl.org/items/510d47df-b79e-a3d9-e040-e00a18064a99.

that conductors and porters complied with the rules that were detailed in company instruction books. These instruction manuals provide interesting insights into how the company created and enforced a racialized hierarchy among its workers.

For example, in 1872, a company mandate suggests that the company was intent on ensuring workers maintained a distinct social boundary between themselves. "Regulations for Porters and Conductors Approved 1872" states in rule number 42 that "personal familiarity between conductors and porters is prohibited" (Pullman Company Archives 05/01/01, Box 2: folder 23). The existence of such a rule suggests that in at least some instances, at least some porters and conductors *had* established "personal familiarity." It appears that the company was interested in creating a clear demarcation between Black porters and White conductors, not only in the division of their labor but also in regard to their interpersonal interactions.

The "Car Service Rules from 1888" codify the hierarchy of manhood in great detail; consider selected instances:

> Article 100. *The Conductor, in addition to his duty of collecting tickets and attending to the other ordinary duties of his position, should as he passes through the several cars that may be under his charge, consider himself an inspector, for the purpose of detecting*
>
> *anything that may be out of order,* and if there is any dust upon the window-sills, or any disorder whatever in the car, he should at once call the attention of the Porter to the improper condition of things . . . In fact, *the Porter should be almost constantly on his feet and working upon the car with a cloth or duster*
>
> Pullman Archives 05/01/01, Box 2: folder 20a. Italics mine.

What is particularly striking about this company rule is that it assumes the porter job will be performed by someone willing to work nonstop without a break. It also structured the job so that it was the job of conductors to point out shortcomings and demand that the porter perform any task the conductor deems necessary. Other rules in this 1888 company manual also reveal the strict hierarchy the company created between "White men's work" and "Black men's work."

> Article 101. (4) *Conductors will be held personally responsible* for the management of cars in their charge, and *have full control and authority over the crew, which will receive orders from them.* They must keep their cars well policed at all times.
>
> (7) *Porters*—The title of Porter in these rules and regulations is used to include also Cooks and Waiters, who are subject to the same rules as porters, so far as the nature of
>
> their respective duties admit. *They are alike subordinate to the conductor, who will maintain with all of them both the business and personal relations that are prescribed for him in regard to porters.* Either porters, cooks, or waiters will perform any service
>
> ordinarily required from but one class of them, when the conductor so directs. If his requirements are thought to be unnecessary, that fact must not prevent *obedience to his orders . . .*
>
> (8) *Gratuities*—Car service men are not permitted to charge or demand from any passenger compensation for service rendered them while on duty. The Porter may, nevertheless, accept, for cleaning boots, or other special service, such remuneration as may be *voluntarily* tendered.
>
> (9) *The Porter's Blanket* will be set apart for his exclusive use. Under no circumstances will he use another, nor will his be given for the use of passengers.

The Berth he occupies will be designated by his superintendent, and he must not, at any time, occupy any other. Porters must be provided with their own *combs* and *hair brushes*, and will not be permitted to use those furnished for passengers' use.

(131. *Blacking Boots*—Porters must clean and polish the boots and shoes of passengers, as also those of their Conductor. Pullman Archives 05/01/01, Box 2: folder 20a. Italics mine..

It can be argued that rule 131, which demanded that porters also clean the shoes of the conductor, was a manifestation of the company providing a "psychological wage" to White workers, as Du Bois ([1935]1995) contended. We should acknowledge that workers being subordinate to the authority of management is a key feature of almost all working relations, past and present. However, these rules take on a racialized and/or gendered dynamic when one group is permanently confined to subordination (Black men) and the other group (White men) is exempt from ever having to be under the dominion of those deemed inherently inferior. These rules establish that Black men are always under the authority of White men on Pullman trains. There is a view of the conductor as a worker trusted to be in charge of and oversee the activities of other workers. This construction of the conductor as someone suited to compel obedience from subordinates excluded women of all races from consideration for the job. Ideology about what group of people are suited for leadership positions has always been a part of the hierarchy established among various persons in the United States (Glenn 2002). Regarding citizenship and labor, White men were viewed as most suited for leadership. Various structures in the United States reflected this notion that White men are superior to women and racial minorities.

White men dominated the courts, politics, education, workplaces, and most social institutions. Even sixty years after the 1964 Civil Rights Act, this group remains overrepresented in key institutions and upper-management roles.

In addition to complying with an abundance of job requirements, porters were also expected to be servants to passengers and perform tasks that they deemed degrading to their "manhood." The presence of company spies on the train meant that Pullman executives and managers were well aware of the degradation that porters endured yet saw fit not to demand more appropriate passenger behavior. It is telling that one of the first demands porters made to the company in 1925 was that they be allowed to wear name tags. This is because it was common practice for passengers to call all porters "George." It has been argued that this practice harkened back to porters being considered "George's (Pullman) boys" (Tye 2004). Also, as late as the 1930s, it was not uncommon for conductors to openly refer to porters as "their boys" (Perata

1996). Porters also report being forced to serve passengers who referred to them as "niggers," to crawl on the ground on all fours, and to allow White children to ride them like animals (Perata 1996).

One other piece of data from this period suggests that the White male managers also saw fit to treat porters as their personal servants. A "letter addressed to all division superintendents. September 19, 1890," titled "Porters Running Errands," reads:

> Dear Sir,
>
> It has come to my notice that District superintendents or their subordinates are in the habit of calling on porters, not assigned to duty but who are reporting for duty, to run errands or to do some work not ordinarily required of porters on duty.
>
> This practice must be discontinued, for the reason that such service constitutes employment and renders the company liable to pay these porters a salary. Please instruct all concerned. -General Superintendent (Pullman Company Archives, Office of the President File (01/01/04 – Volume 6).

This letter demonstrates that it was part of the workplace culture to treat porters as inferiors. Furthermore, this letter highlights that the company's objections to treating porters this way did not revolve around affording them the respect White men were entitled to. Rather, the company's concern was purely financial—in this instance, an attempt to not be liable for paying porters extra wages.

Explaining Why Only Black Men Were Porters

One of the most striking features regarding how Pullman constructed the porter job is the extent to which its social construction of Black manhood seems alien in the contemporary context. Black men as appropriate workers to provide childcare to White children. Black men as not sexually threatening and therefore appropriate workers to be trusted to work in the personal sleeping quarters of White women. Black men as the ideal personal service workers. Black men being trusted to know "their place" and keep quiet about abuse from Whites. These constructions of Black manhood that were at the center of how the Pullman Company structured the porter job seem absolutely foreign. But for three or four generations, these constructions were some of the most widely held in society as a whole, and the Pullman porter job was a key to creating, publicizing, and maintaining this construction.

The creation of the distinct job category "porter" on Pullman trains in 1867 appears to coincide with two key factors—the introduction of the company's first trains that included luxurious dining options and the looming completion of the transcontinental railroad two years later, in 1869. In 1867,

George Pullman introduced the first sleeping car, the *president,* with a kitchen attached. Seat-side service, offering 131 dining options, was provided to passengers for the first time. A year later, the *Delmonico,* the first train car dedicated exclusively to fine dining, was also added to the Pullman brand, which had become synonymous with luxurious rail travel. Prior to these dining-sleeping cars, passengers had to either pack a meal from home or hurriedly consume a meal at a railroad eating house during the approximately twenty minutes the train was parked at the station. With the inception of food service on the trains came the need for additional workers to serve passengers food. The other development that intensified the labor needs aboard trains was the completion of the transcontinental railroad and the Pullman Company's ability to sign leases to service these tracks in 1869. Unlike previous journeys, which lasted a day or two, transcontinental trips took six days of constant travel. This extended period of travel placed even greater demands on those taking care of passenger needs.

Freemen Yet Slaves under "Abe" Lincoln's Son, written by a Pullman porter, C. F Anderson, in 1904, provides a window into understanding just how taxing these extended trips were on porters. On a five-day/four-night trip from Chicago to Oakland, Anderson was allowed a total of ten hours off during the entire trip. He wrote,

> it frequently happens that we are on duty forty-eight or even sixty hours without rest, and yet we are expected to look fresh and be just as attentive as if we had taken our regular rest, as our all-wise creator intended. (Anderson 1904, 26–27)

Various other accounts from porters verify that such practices were widespread, although "official" company policy in 1874 stated that porters were guaranteed a rest period from 10 p.m. to 3 a.m. This policy was meaningless in practice. Porters were not even guaranteed a quiet place to sleep, often being relegated to the smoking room, which also doubled as the men's bathroom. In practice, this meant that porters slept (or tried to) behind a curtain in the men's bathroom. They also encountered passengers coming and leaving all night to use the restroom, light a cigar, drink, play cards, and share stories with other passengers. These disruptions to the porters' attempts to sleep were further complicated by two other factors. First, even as late as 1925, Pullman Company Instructions to Porters explicitly demanded that "under no circumstances will the porter request passengers to vacate the smoking room so that he may retire." Second, the company demanded that porters be on call all night long. In practice, this meant that when passengers rang a bell in the middle of the night, it was the responsibility of the porter to attend to their needs, even if this occurred during what was ostensibly their "sleep time." "Doubling back" or "doubling out" was a third way in which porters' labor was constructed by the company as the "constant, consummate servant." This management practice meant that without any prior notice, a porter, just ending one cross-country trip, could be forced by the company to immediately turn around and begin working on another cross-country trip (Derickson 2008). This assured that the porter had no time to stop and rest before having to begin the arduous labor of preparing another sleeping car for a long trip.

Why were White men considered inappropriate for such work? Perhaps the most obvious argument, and the one most widely held for such cases in general, is that who was hired simply reflected the availability of a labor force and the character of the preexisting racial-gender division of labor. The census data for Illinois and Chicago make it clear that the choice of Black men for the job was anything but obvious and was certainly not based on their constituting the largest pool of available labor (see tables 2.1 and 2.2).

These data demonstrate that it was not their plentiful labor supply that made Black men "natural" choices for the porter job. Also, the 1860 census identifies 25,646 individuals who were classified as personal servants. Ten years later, this number had risen to 44,903 in the state of Illinois and 12,279 personal servants in the city of Chicago. So, even if one assumes (illogically)

Table 2.1 Illinois and Chicago Population in 1860

	Illinois Population	*% of Illinois Population*	*Chicago Population*	*% of Chicago Population*
Total	1,711,951	-----	109,260	100
White	1,704,291	99.5	108,215	99
Irish Foreign-Born	87,573	5.1	19,889	18
Colored	7,628	0.004	955	0.008

Source: U.S. Eighth Census (1860) "Population" data. "White" includes both native-born and foreign-born. "Colored" includes both "Black" and "mulatto" in the 1860 census.

Table 2.2 Illinois and Chicago Population in 1870

	Illinois Population	*% of Illinois Population*	*Chicago Population*	*% of Chicago Population*
Total	2,539,891		298,977	100
White	2,511,096	98.8	295,281	98.8
Irish Foreign-Born	120,162	4.7	39,988	13.7
Colored	28,762	0.011	3,691	0.012

Source: Ninth Census (1870) "Populations" sections. "White" includes both native-born and foreign-born. "Colored" includes both "Black" and "mulatto" in the 1860 census. In 1870, the Chicago census "colored" included "Black," "mulatto" and "four Indians."

that every single "colored" person in the state and/or city of Chicago was employed as a servant, it would remain that the vast majority of those working as servants would still be White!

One explanation for why White men and women were not hired for these jobs is that White people are inherently unsuited to service. The best-known book about Pullman car porters comes close to making exactly this argument. Tye (2004) argues that it was only "natural" that eventually White men would be replaced because "Caucasian men were neither trained nor disposed to do the humble work of valet, bellhop, maid, and janitor" (23). Tye (2004) posits that in order to distinguish Pullman cars from others, George Pullman decided to focus on providing superior service and that this necessitated "hiring personnel whose sole devotion was to unhesitating service" (23).

In fact, White men were not inherently unsuited for personal service work. Ethnic "White" Irish men had a history of working in the hotel industry (Nichols 1874). Irish men were viewed as suited to watering work, which is a key element of the porter job (Nichols 1874; Sandoval-Strausz 2007), so why not hire them to serve on the train? Furthermore, there was also a population of Irish immigrant men in the city of Chicago during the 1860s. At least one manager, Duane Doty, Pullman town manager, viewed the Irish as not particularly suited to manufacturing work. This raises the question of why Irish men were not hired as porters. They had experience in the occupation of personal service. Importantly, Irish men were a plentiful labor source in Chicago, unlike Black men, who represented less than 1 percent of the city's population in 1867. So why weren't Irish men tapped for this newly created job?

In retrospect, it might seem natural that women of all races would be excluded from working as porters on the train. It is reasonable to assume that prevailing ideology would dictate that women who spent the night serving single men alcohol and working in their sleeping quarters would become a stigmatized group for compromising their "virtue." One could argue that, of course, a luxury brand would not want to be represented by women who were viewed as sexually promiscuous.

However, there are several phenomena that challenge this argument. First, while the exact date of the introduction of maids (all Black women) to the train remains unclear, less than thirty years after the introduction of the Black porter, it was deemed appropriate by the company that Black women be suitable for overnight service trips. Scouring the archival material reveals there were *no* company regulations that maids be guaranteed protection from sexual abuse or even guaranteed an assigned sleeping berth away from male passengers. Second, there was a history of women working in taverns until the wee hours of the morning, serving single, drunk men. Third, it was not uncommon for White women to work as in-home servants. Fourth, given the emerging ideology in the South that Black men were innately a sexual threat to White women, one could also argue that it was "rational" that Pullman would not trust Black men to work in the intimate quarters of White women. In contrast to Southern views about Black men and Western/Hawaiian views of certain Asian men as sexual predators, White men were conceptualized as being rational and in control of their desires. Therefore, in many ways, it makes more sense that White men would have been tapped as "suitable" workers for the porter job.

The available data do not seem to be strong enough to reach a definitive conclusion about why Black men became porters, but the data *do* seem to make it clear that it was a decision by George Pullman, not White workers. Unlike the first conductor, next to nothing is known about the first porter Pullman hired. One thing is certain: the first porter was a Black man. In response to a lawsuit filed 100 years after the first porters rode the trains, the Pullman Company acknowledged that they had never hired a White man or woman to work as porters. From the beginning and throughout, the porter was clearly racialized as a job not suited or appropriate for White men and women. At least initially, the job did not acquire its racial-gender character as a result of struggles between various groups of workers but rather as a result of a decision by the employer.

The Pullman Company created a new job, but they drew upon slavery-era ideology that conceptualized Black men as suitable for personal service and caretaking. A very influential essay of the era that was later reprinted as an appendix to *The Dred Scott Decision* explains this perspective in detail. Just two years before Pullman built his first sleeping car, and just ten years before the first Pullman car porter was hired, Samuel A. Cartwright, a physician and pro-slavery advocate from Louisiana, wrote:

> The importance of having these particular employments, regarded as servile and degrading by the White man, attended to by the Black race, whose instincts are not repugnant to them, will be at once apparent to all. *There is no office which the negro or mulatto covets more than that of being a body servant to a real gentleman.* There is no office which gives him such a high opinion of himself, and it is utterly impossible for him to attach the idea of degradation to it. North or South, free or slave, they are ever at the elbow, behind the table, in hotels and steamboats; ever ready, with brush in hand, to brush the coat or Black the shoes, or to perform any menial service which may be required, and to hold out the open palm for the dime. The innate love to act as body servant or lacquey is too strongly developed in the negro race to be concealed. (Ruchames 1969, 471)

This perspective of Black manhood as inherently servile was reproduced on the Pullman trains. As will be discussed in the following chapter, the company marketed this image of the Black man as a happy servant to the

American public. Not only were Black men supposedly elated to serve others in return for a meager tip, but they also had to be conceptualized as safe and trustworthy around women. Although Blacks were often referred to as "savages," there was an element of Southern racial thought that conceptualized Black men as being suited to take care of White women and children while the White men were away. These internal contradictions were and are certainly no impediment to anti-Black racism.

Utilizing the Revolutionary War experience as a prime example, Cartwright notes that when White men went off to fight the British, they left "their wives and children, their old men and cripples, for seven long years, *to their negroes to take care of*" (Ruchames 1969, 475). He goes on to argue that enslaved Black people never deserted their responsibilities to the White families that they served. When enemy soldiers were nearby, Cartwright contends that enslaved Black men would protect their White mistress and her children at all costs. In his view, enslaved Whites, Indians, or any other race would have killed the mistress and children. Only the slavish Black person could be trusted to care for the family while White male authority was absent. Contrary to the view that would develop after slavery that Black men were an inherent threat to White women's purity—this perspective articulated a few years before the civil war conceptualizes Black men as inherently servile and trustworthy regarding the caretaking of White women and children. There is at least suggestive evidence that Pullman himself subscribed to similar views. At a time when most of his neighbors, the aristocrats of Prairie Avenue, "would only consider English servants," Pullman chose instead to hire "a Negro coachman and Black domestics" for his family and business excursions (Tye 2004, 26).

One might argue that porters were the lowest-paid employees in the Pullman Company because their labor generated the least amount of surplus value for the company. However, data from 1893 demonstrate that the company generated far greater income from the operation of sleeping cars versus their manufacture. Of the 11 million dollars in total company earnings, 9 million was generated from the operation of sleeping cars (Buder 1967, 134).

The company itself acknowledged that it did not pay Black men a "living wage" that they clearly felt (at least in principle) White men were entitled to. This notion that Black men and their families were not deserving of a living wage was part of the larger racist ideology at the time, which posited that Black families (and other minorities) warranted lower wages because they could innately live on less money (Glenn 2002). In 1890, a group of porters in Chicago requested a minimum wage of $40 a month so that they would not have to rely on tips to survive. In response to this demand for a modicum of racial equality on the trains, an unnamed company official informed reporters that the company felt "there will be a chance to do away with the tipping evil. We would pay the White porters living wages if the 'coon' wants to go for good, all he has to do is strike" an executive was reported as saying in the *Chicago Herald* July 14, 1890 article (Hirsch 2003, 15). This quote reflects the dominant racial ideology, which devalued Black individuals and families. It appears that *because* the porter job was a "Black man's job" (in theory and practice), it was viewed as inherently deserving of lower remuneration than that of a "White man's job," which merited a living wage.

It is hard to argue that organized White labor was the reason Black men were initially hired as Pullman porters and continued to be relegated to such work during this era. Conductors at the Pullman Company were not organized during this period. The Sleeping Car Conductors' Union was not founded until 1918 and only had contracts with the Pullman Company starting in 1922 (Northrup 1944, 76).

CONCLUSION

Understanding the origins of racial-gender inequality within an organization is critical for theorizing which factors play a role in the establishment of workplace hierarchies. Specifically, the initial question of this chapter regards why and how the porter job came to be held by only Black men and the conductor job held only by White men. It has been argued that it was only "natural" that Pullman executives (most notably George Pullman, who founded the company) would choose Black men and Black men only to work as porters (Tye 2004). In the most well-known book on Pullman porters, *Rising from the Rails,* Tye argues that it was "natural" that George Pullman would select only former house slaves for the servile and degrading porter job because no White man would ever take such work. However, there is nothing that is particularly "natural," inevitable, or predetermined about establishing racialized inequality. In many instances, it is quite possible that financial elites could have made various other decisions. There were no particular reasons why White men could not be constructed as suitable servants. In fact, elite Whites in Chicago almost exclusively employed White men and women as butlers and maids (Tye 2004). Also, between 1865 and 1867 (before the porter job category was created in the company), White male conductors handled passengers' personal needs. Irish men, in particular, had a history of working in the hotel industry and the waitering profession (Nichols 1874; Sandoval-Strausz 2007). Additionally, by selecting Black men over Irish men for the porter job, the Pullman Company was not responding to the local labor market supply. As census data demonstrates, in 1860 and 1870, Blacks represented a minuscule portion of the population in Chicago. A desire for "super-exploitable" labor is readily apparent. Although one cannot be certain about George Pullman's racial ideology, in later years, there *is* data reflecting company executives' racial ideology. That will be the focus of the following chapter.

Chapter 3

Pullman Executives' Public and Private Racial Discourse, 1890s–1950s

It is perhaps plausible to claim that the original decision to hire only Black porters might have been based on a purely economic rationale, but this chapter demonstrates that company executives justified the persistence of this practice by explicitly attaching racial meanings to the porter job and enforcing strict social boundaries between Black and White workers. The data reveal these actions were not a result of pressure from White workers and were not merely a result of employers' desire to divide and conquer workers through a system of racialized paternalism. Rather, the racial hierarchies on Pullman trains reflected company executives' own beliefs about Blackness and White supremacy. Employers' racial ideology was a causal agent in the relegation of Black workers to the least desirable jobs on the train. How company executives continued to racialize the porter job as "Black man's work" and the conductor job as "White man's work" in *public discourse and private communications* is the focus of this chapter. The data demonstrates that both publicly and privately, Pullman Company executives conceived of Blacks and Whites as inherently different and explicitly continued to imbue work on the trains with racist meanings. Indeed, the most crystal clear racializations of the porter job appear in the *private* internal communications between company executives.

Although the porter job was constructed by company executives as a "Black man's job," it is necessary to understand that the racialized workplace hierarchy company executives created and legitimized on Pullman trains was not uncommon for this time period. In fact, one of the most interesting aspects of the Pullman case is that, in many regards, it provided one of the very best jobs Black men could obtain at this time. Analytically, it is critical to note that even in the "best-case scenario" for Black men in this era, they were relegated to the most degrading work. While the practice of hiring Black men as porters did provide them with an opportunity to earn incomes above the average wages of Black men, they were confined to being the "perfect servant."

Gathering data on employers' racial ideology presents certain challenges. Racial ideology is often taken for granted and therefore not explicitly articulated (Myers and Williamson 2001). For this chapter, I analyzed congressional testimony provided by Pullman company executives about working conditions onboard, as well as all surviving internal company memos regarding work on the trains, all of the company-produced *Pullman News* publications, and all the detailed porter and conductor disciplinary files available in the company archives for the years 1894–1965 were among my data sources. The public and private discourse among company executives was incredibly consistent. Black people were racialized in public and internal communications as being particularly suited for servitude.

By 1900, the Pullman company maintained a monopoly in the sleeping car service on U.S. railroads. In the 1920s, porters' status on the trains remained the same as when the job was created in 1867. Porters were still paid significantly less than conductors. For example, in 1915, porters earned a base salary of $27.50 in comparison to conductors, who received a base rate of $70 a month. Sleep conditions had not improved on the train, and porters on average still got three to four hours of sleep a night (Derickson 2008). Porters were still required to be at the beck and call of passengers around the clock. They continued to shine everyone's shoes, serve passengers food, clean up after customers, awake in the middle of the night to respond to a passenger ringing the bell and demanding a glass of water, make beds, babysit children, and attend to drunken passengers—all in return for a tip. Because porters' wages were so low, they had to rely on tipping in order to make a decent living. In this sense, company executives structured the porter's job so that his ability to earn a living wage was inextricably linked to his ability to be a humble servant.

Notably, the Pullman Company paid porters these low wages in spite of being a highly profitable company. In 1915, the company's finances were disclosed in public testimony provided by Robert Todd Lincoln, the late president's son. At this time, Lincoln was the chairman of the board of directors. He was president of the Pullman Co. from the time shortly after the death of Mr. Pullman, in October 1897, until May 11, 1911, when he retired on account of ill health. Lincoln testified that the company had a capital stock of $120 million dollars, with no bonded indebtedness, and had paid dividends of eight percent per annum since 1900 (Report of Commission of on Industrial Relations 1915, 9964–9966).

Given this high and consistent level of profitability, hiring and paying decisions were not dictated by economic necessity. These decisions flow more from employers' race-gender ideology, which was revealed in the ways company executives articulated their views about the difference between the conductor and porter jobs. Because company executives' race-gender ideology contributed to the marginalization of Black workers on Pullman trains, this chapter devotes significant attention to analyzing the racial discourse espoused by top officials at the Pullman Company regarding their employees.

In describing the nature of the conductor job, the following testimony was provided to the 1915 Industrial Relations Commission by L. S. Hungerford, the general manager of the Pullman Company, regarding the conductor job:

> Chairman WALSH. Please state the method by which your conductors are employed.
>
> Mr. HUNGERFORD. The conductors we are in receipt of a great many applications. In fact, I think we have got thousands of them on file now. Those men, generally, where they can, present themselves to representatives at the various points, who interview them, look up the letters that are submitted by them—such letters as they care to submit from people endorsing them, and they are taken up when the vacancies [arise, occur?]
>
> Chairman WALSH. Well, what training is given Pullman conductors?
>
> Mr. HUNGERFORD. That is one thing about our service—it does not require trained men. He does not have to go through any special school. If he is careful, intelligent, and courteous, he will have no difficulty in carrying on the work without any special training. He is allowed 10 days' time in which he receives full pay to go through what we call a course of instruction. We have instructors at various large centers that post him in regard to the detailed duty, and he is sent out on a line with old conductors, and then put on a light line. It is not a difficult position. (Report of Commission on Industrial Relations 1915, 9551)

Strikingly, the higher wages paid to conductors are not presented as a result of their job requiring specialized skills or the difficulty of the position. Hungerford's commentary on the porter job is similarly elucidating.

Under questioning by Chairman Walsh, General Manager Hungerford had active recruitment operations in the South to "get men of a desirable class," including students for the summer months. The company found a plentiful supply: "I don't think there is any point where we cannot get porters except on the Pacific Coast" (9553). The problem was not in total supply, but in getting men "of the right caliber"; recruitment emphasized the South because the company thought it got "better" (read: servile) men from there.

Chairman WALSH. Is that the idea, that you get men that will serve better; that is, that makes better servants than the colored men in the North?

Mr. HUNGERFORD. Well, we find that their training there better fits them for service on the car.

Chairman WALSH. How do they compare those colored men that are not found in the slums how do they compare with the Negro you get in the South?

Mr. HUNGERFORD. I think the old southern colored man makes the best porter on the car.

Chairman WALSH. Well, in what way?

Mr. HUNGERFORD. Well, because he is more adapted to waiting on the passengers and gives them better attention and has a better manner, that is more acceptable to them and more pleasant.

Porters were given unpaid training on the cars. According to Mr. Hungerford, "It don't take more than two or three days for any intelligent fellow to learn to do it." It is important to note that the company publicly differentiated between "types" of Blacks. Company executives publicly stated that Black men from the southern United States were deemed more appropriate servants than their northern counterparts.

There are numerous ways in which the company racialized employment on trains so that conductors were afforded both a material and "psychological" wage as White men and Black men were denied such benefits as porters. These various elements of racializing the conductor and porter jobs are illustrated in greater detail throughout this chapter. However, let us begin by discussing the wage differentials between conductors and porters based on publicly disclosed data from the 1915 Commission on Industrial Relations (see table 3.1).

Table 3.1 1915 Monthly Wage Schedule for Conductors and Porters

Duration of Employment	*Conductors*	*Porters*
Starting	$70	$27.50
After 6 months	$75	$27.50
After 1 year	$80	$27.50
After 2 years	$85	$27.50
After 5 years	$90	$27.50
After 10 years	$95	$27.50
After 15 years	No data provided	$28.87

Source: RCIR, Pullman Exhibits—Appendix A.

In addition to being guaranteed a family wage, White men were also afforded an opportunity to increase their salaries over time. On the other hand, Black men were confined to a job that was a dead end in terms of wage increases.

Wage rates have not necessarily been determined simply by economic calculations but have historically been shaped by subjective/ideological notions of an appropriate wage for certain groups (Kessler-Harris 1991). In the post–Reconstruction Era, White men were deemed worthy of a "man's wage," which was enough to support a worker and his family at a decent standard. Black men, on the other hand, were not deemed worthy of a "man's wage" sufficient to support a family for several reasons. First, Black women were viewed as laborers and expected to help support their families. Black men were not expected to support a non-working wife.

Second, widely held racial ideology stated that people of color could survive on very little because they were less evolved (Glenn 2002, 82). Although porters were able to supplement their wages through tips from satisfied passengers, several factors about conductors versus porters' remuneration remain important to remember. First, conductors enjoyed "fixed" wages, unlike porters, who received low wages regardless of how many or few passengers they could potentially garner tips from. Second, unlike contemporary tipping relationships, porters were in contact with customers for hours and days on end. The duration of the trip, along with the varied requests, from fetching water in the middle of the night to babysitting children, created more uncertainty in the worker-customer relationship. Lastly, porters' tips were contingent upon them fulfilling racialized ideals about Blacks' servility.

PENSIONS

Another reflection of Black men being denied a "man's wage" are the pensions the Pullman company paid to various workers. I read all the available transcripts of Pullman "Executive Committee Meetings" that were available in the archive (1897–1913). Created in 1897 shortly after the death of George Pullman, the Executive Committee was responsible for determining which workers were deserving of a pension/death benefit to family and what amount would be paid by the company. President Robert Todd Lincoln, the personnel director, and three other company executives received pension/death benefit requests from district superintendents for workers employed for thirty years or more. Unfortunately, there is no data regarding why and how company executives decided which amounts were appropriate for various groups of

Table 3.2 Monthly Pensions of Pullman Employees, 1904

Occupation	*Race-Gender*	*Monthly Pension*
Commissary Officer	White Men	$133.33
Conductor	White Men	$40
Seamstress	White Women	$25
Porter	Black Men	$12.50

Source: Pullman Archive 02/01/02—Volume 15.
*Commissary officers were responsible for overseeing that conductors and porters-in-charge turned in the ticket fare stubs and the exact amount of money to the company at various train stops.

workers. The data simply states a potential pensioner's name, occupation, and benefit levels.

Table 3.2 shows the monthly pension allowance of various Pullman workers in 1904:

It is noteworthy that retired Black men are expected to survive on half the pension of White women. In 1913, the company established a Pension Plan to be administered by the Board of Pensions, which comprised five officers appointed by the president. This difference between monthly pensions for conductors and porters would persist throughout the existence of the Pullman Company (Hirsch 2003). Company executives would also demonstrate racialized ideology regarding the porter job in their public discourse.

Race in Public Discourse

This section examines the Pullman Company's pronouncements about the porter and conductor jobs in public commentary. The data utilized for this section include company advertising materials, the company-produced *Pullman News* magazine, and testimony from Pullman company executives L. S. Hungerford and Robert Todd Lincoln to the 1915 "Congressional Commission on Industrial Relations" regarding the work conditions of the porters and conductors. Several themes emerge in these data that indicate Pullman company executives explicitly racialized the porter job as work suited for Black men.

Porters Are Depicted as Safe and "Happy Servants" in Advertising and Popular Culture

The porter job would continue to be publicly racialized as a "Black man's job." By the 1920s, 12,000 Pullman porters provided personal service to the over 35 million passengers that slept on Pullman cars each year. Pullman Company was the single largest employer of Black men in the country (Bates-Tompkins 2001). One key reason why Pullman had managed to attract so many customers was the level of luxurious service the company advertised could only be provided on a Pullman sleeper by a Pullman porter. In this regard, the Pullman sleeping car "addressed not merely passengers' need for rest but for their psychological preference for luxury as well" (Arnesen 2001, 18). The Pullman company had a flair for advertising and widely disseminated the cultural image of the smiling Black male porter, happy to tend to all of the passengers' needs (Reiff and Hirsch 1989). The image of the happy servile Black male porter became a part of American popular culture. For example, the 1927 silent movie *The Girl on the Pullman* depicted a porter bowing and grinning widely while receiving a tip from a customer (Bates-Tompkins 2001).

Within company publications, porters are depicted as happy servants in public racial discourse. The image of the grinning porter below appears in the December 1924 edition of Pullman News. The company reprinted the image and story from a previous edition of *The*

Nation's Business

The caption reads "*An Innocent Abroad: He Gets Homesick for a Pullman Car and 'George'.*" (See figure 3.1.)

This article chronicles the travels of Henry Schott through Europe on poorly equipped railroad services, including shoddy food, uncomfortable sleeping quarters, and a lack of personal service. The author laments that

Figure 3.1 An Innocent Abroad. *Source*: Pullman News, December, 1924. Courtesy Newberry Library.

on European trains, conductors (White men) are the only employees on the train. He writes,

> "And while we are on the topic of sleeping cars, they have fixed the amount of the tip to be paid to the conductor, who also acts as porter and waiter, bringing your coffee to your compartment in the morning. You are by posted rule of the sleeping car company asked to pay the conductor-porter-waiter 10 percent of your combined railways and sleeping car fares."

The article later goes on to sing the praises of Pullman service and the great "cheerful" service rendered by "George" (the Pullman porter) in America. Two layers of racial ideology are reflected in this image. First, the White conductor is deemed worthy of a man-to-man handshake and the exchanging of cigars. Second, the porter is pictured as grinning ear to ear, happy to receive a tip for his unflagging service. It is implicitly argued by the company that if tips/income for train service workers are fixed, then they will be less likely to render the round-the-clock personal service Pullman company executives required of porters and maids. The European model, whereby one employee is responsible for providing all train service, illustrates that alternative workplace models were available to the Pullman company. Instead of dividing train service labor in a manner where White male conductors were supervisors and Black male porters were servants—it is possible that the company could have opted for an all-White workforce that would be responsible for all the train service work; an all-Black workforce that would perform conductor's work in addition to personal service; or a bi-racial workforce of conductor-porters.

This full-page article in Pullman News literally refers to a porter as "The World's Most Perfect Servant" (see figure 3.2) and celebrates the fact he has been *confined to servitude for forty-five years.*

The image of the cheerful, perfect servant would be replicated in the company's advertising campaigns. Porters are portrayed as gleeful to serve passengers at their beck and call. Although conductors are deemed ultimately responsible for the quality of personal service rendered by Black employees, these White men are not depicted as happy servants. Conductors are service workers, but they are primarily supervisors on the train to ensure that Black workers comply with passengers' service demands.

The company's promotion practices reflect the notion that conductors are viewed as appropriate supervisors. Pictures of all the company executives were routinely displayed in the Pullman News. Data gathered from these pictures from 1922 until the paper stopped being published in 1955 demonstrate that all the images of company executives and managers during this period appear to be White men. From the existing data, it appears that porters were clearly excluded from the ranks of management in the company. On the other hand, a study conducted by the company and prominently placed

December, 1922

Here Is World's Most Perfect Servant

Porter David G. Scott, In Nearly 45 Years Service, Did Not Receive a Demerit Mark or Complaint

THE 9,000-odd porters in the Pullman service are sources of great pride to the Company. Manifestly some are better than others, and incidents in the careers of many of these have been chronicled in THE PULLMAN NEWS. One of those whose achievements have yet to be set forth is David G. Scott, retired, of Los Angeles, dean of the corps diplomatique, who during his 44½ years of continuous Pullman service received 476 credit marks and not one demerit. The "Admirable Crichton" at his best could learn from Porter Scott, whose career stamps him as being the world's most perfect example of good service and courtesy.

A porter receives merits and demerits largely upon the reports made by traveling inspectors, most of whom are not known to him. Passengers' praise and complaints also figure, naturally. He is commended for cleanliness, willingness and expert service. He may receive black marks for discourtesy or untidiness in various forms. He may not remove soiled towels or keep the clean supply replenished. He may step on the plush seats in making down an upper berth. Or in putting away an upper he may blur the polished surface by failing to place a cloth under his hand.

Today, in his seventy-seventh year, Porter Scott is sunning his declining years in Los Angeles, but ready to respond to an emergency call for porters. He has kept his last uniform in excellent shape, and, like an old fire horse, feels that he has a few good trips left in him. Rheuma-

DAVID G. SCOTT

faithful service. He never received a cross word from a passenger, he says, and associate old time porters say he was the "champion dirt and dust chaser." His car was "Spotless Town" on wheels.

Although a porter on a tourist car receives a higher wage than one assigned to a standard sleeper, the former branch is viewed askance, to put it mildly. Oftentimes porters are disciplined by being transferred from standard lines to the tourists. But Porter Scott preferred the latter.

The heterogeneous element often found on tourist sleepers had no terrors for "Dave." The more women and children there were the merrier was the journey. He turned every trip into a house party of unparalleled gaiety and content. Most porters find gratuities scant on tourist lines. That was not the experience of the genial diplomat Scott. Early on one trip a woman passenger sought to tip Scott a quarter for some service.

"No, no, ma'am," said Scott, protestingly. "Don't you give this now. You keep it and give it ALL to me at the end of the trip." Scott was a psychologist.

This retired veteran was born in 1846 in Midway, Woodford county, Kentucky, and was reared on his father's farm. When the Civil war broke out he enlisted in the Union army and saw three years' active service under Col. W. W. Woodward. In May, 1870, when 24, he entered the Pullman service at Houston, Tex., then only an agency, serving under Agents De Pue, Harrison and Fairweather. For

Figure 3.2 The World's Most Perfect Servant. *Source*: Pullman News. December, 1922. Courtesy Newberry Library.

in the Pullman News asserted that between 1934 and 1955, about 75 percent of company executives and management had formerly worked as Pullman conductors. Compare this to the predicament of Black male workers, which Lincoln admitted to in his congressional testimony:

> Commissioner WEINSTOCK. Let me ask you what opportunity, if any, is there for advancement? What opportunity, for example, of a negro [*sic*] porter who shows very high efficiency? Is there any provision . . .

> Mr. LINCOLN (interrupting). There is no provision in our service, sir. we have no place to put him.
>
> Commissioner WEINSTOCK. So it is sort of what is known as a blind alley job? Mr. LINCOLN. Yes, sir.

In this instance, a company executive is publicly stating that even the most talented, highly efficient Black workers were not provided with any opportunity for advancement. In addition to the conductor job providing White men with a fixed family wage, it also afforded them an opportunity for career advancement and greater wealth. So, although the Pullman company did hire more Black men than any other employer in the 1920s, it did so in a way that relegated them to the dead-end porter job, which necessitated perpetual servitude in return for tips in order to provide a living wage.

The company's *Conductors Instruction Book* from 1926 displays this racialized hierarchy explicitly:

> Conductors have jurisdiction over all other car employees on cars under their charge and are held responsible for the proper performance of their duties. If unable to exact obedience, a report giving the facts must be made to the District Superintendent. It is their duty. . . to supervise the service and enforce observance by subordinate car employees.

The instruction manuals for porters, maids, and attendants (all Black workers, with the exception of some Filipino club car attendants) also include the exact same wording, reinforcing that they are subordinate employees who must obey the instructions of the White male conductor. In private company memoranda and disciplinary records (discussed later), Pullman executives further clarify what *type* of Black worker they desire. The characteristics desired in porters—subservience, knowing "their place," and happiness serving others—were antithetical to the company-espoused notions of White manhood.

The employers' construction of servitude as the exclusive domain of Black men was a causal factor in relegating Blacks to the porter job. While economic calculations certainly played a role in the Pullman Company's practice of hiring only Black men (cheap labor) as porters, deeply held beliefs about innate racial differences also contributed to the creation and maintenance of a deeply hierarchical workplace.

Prevailing contemporary stereotypes would lead us to expect that in a company that employed White men (conductors), Black men (porters), and Black women (maids) to provide personal service to passengers in their sleeping quarters, Black men would be the group least publicly identified as being in close contact with White women. The opposite is the case.

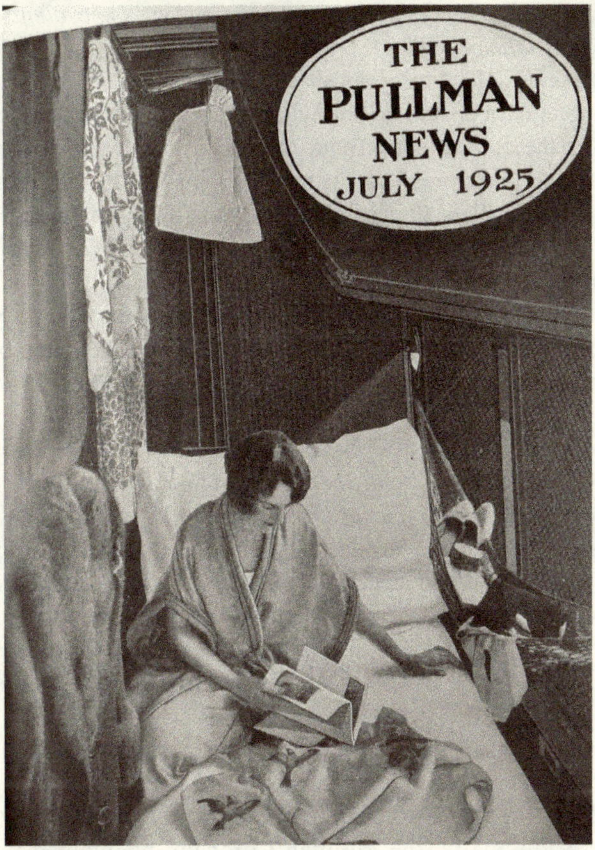

Figure 3.3 A Fair Lady in Her Sleeper. *Source*: Pullman News, July, 1925. Courtesy Newberry Library.

"A Fair Passenger" depicts an image (see figure 3.3) from the Pullman News in May 1930 and is one of several that, while they do not depict a porter, show single White female passengers in their nightgowns. These pictures alert the viewer that White women will be in this position on the Pullman sleeping cars, that their Black male porter might be beckoned in the middle of the night to bring water or an extra blanket, and that even though this is the case—no sexual misconduct will occur.

That porters were not deemed sexual threats, and this benefited Black men in terms of being able to secure work. On one hand, it could be argued that by allowing Black men to work as porters, the Pullman company was not racist toward Black workers. Indeed, the company could have taken the path of excluding Black workers from work on the trains. The practice of maintaining this job monopoly for Black men is best described as "*benevolent-exploitative racialized paternalism*," that is, organizing work along racial lines but providing workers of color with jobs that the employer deems they are "lucky to have." The employer utilizes the wider racism in society at large to paint themselves as the benevolent provider of employment for workers of color. Furthermore, the widespread racial ideology that Blacks were inferior and suited for serving others underpinned Pullman's employment practices on the trains.

In the Pullman case, the company constructed itself as a philanthropist to the wider Black community and the wellbeing of porters. Aspects of this "benevolent-exploitative racialized paternalism" are articulated by company executives in their committee meetings. The Executive Committee was created by the new president of the company, Robert Todd Lincoln, in 1897. The Committee was composed of President Robert Todd Lincoln, the personnel director, and three other company executives appointed by Lincoln. I read all the transcripts of Pullman "Executive Committee Meetings" that were available in the archive (1897–1913). In later years, only agendas for the meetings exist in the archive. In these meetings, company executives decided wages for different workers, how much and which workers were worthy of a pension and/or death benefits, and which charitable contributions to make. During these years, 1897–1913, the company listed only four charitable donations (see table 3.3).

Of all (based on available data) the charitable contributions made by the Executive Committee, the donation toward the construction of Wabash YMCA, which provided housing for Black men in Chicago, is by far the largest. Additionally, the Pullman Company maintained ties with the Black community and provided financial support for several organizations involved in improving the welfare of African Americans in the Chicago area.

Table 3.3 Pullman Company Charitable Donations, 1897–1913

Organization	*Purpose of Donation*	*Total Amount*
First Calvary Illinois National Guard	no reason provided	$3,700
Order of Railway Conductors	"1913 National Convention"	$100
Chicago Association of Commerce Relief	"benefits for flood sufferers"	$2,500
Chicago YMCA Board of Trustees	"to aid in the creation of an Association building for the benefit of colored men and boys"	$10,000

Source: Pullman files 02/01/02, Volume 15.

Bates-Tompkins (2001) provides the most comprehensive analysis of Pullman Company paternalism in the Southside Chicago Black community and its role in undermining community support for organizing efforts on behalf of porters. Although from 1897 to 1913 only this one (very substantial) donation to the Black community was made by the Pullman Company, during his tenure as president of the company, George Pullman was a benefactor to numerous organizations in the Black community. In 1891, George Pullman and his daughter Florence provided significant financial support for the construction of Provident Hospital, which served Black patients and employed Black doctors and nurses (Bates-Tompkins, 43). After the formation of the Chicago Urban League in 1915 (two years after the period covered by the extant minutes of the Executive Committee), this organization continued to receive substantial contributions from the Pullman Company (Bates-Tompkins, 44–45). These paternalistic efforts included donating money to local Black politicians such as Edward H. Wright, a lawyer, and Chicago's first Black ward committeeman. However, the most important aspect of Pullman company paternalism in Chicago's Black community revolved around its long-term relationship with the city's largest African Methodist Episcopal (AME) Church and its Reverend Archibald James Carey. Reverend Carey's ascent to being both a spiritual and political force in the Black community was helped in large part by contributions from the Pullman Company. These contributions to Carey and the AME Church helped support the nursery and kindergarten for the children of working mothers. The AME Church also served other functions that were not necessarily related to religion. At Carey's church, newly arrived Black residents also received information on where to obtain employment. Additionally, Reverend Carey would announce job openings at Pullman from the pulpit, and he was a key referral for Blacks who sought employment as car cleaners in the Pullman Chicago yards (Bates-Tompkins, 45–48).

These paternalistic efforts were underscored by the idea that the Pullman Company, although confining Black employees to serving as porters and maids on the train, was at least providing them with the "opportunity" to work that was denied them in other industries. Lincoln articulates this "benevolent-exploitative racialized paternalism" during his congressional testimony.

> Chairman WALSH. Do you consider $27.50 a month sufficient to enable a negro [*sic*] porter to maintain himself and family in comfort and decency?
>
> Mr. LINCOLN. *The colored race, as we know, were subject to great limitations in the past to obtain employment in this country, and I believe as a matter of fact that outside of what you might call the learned professions that they got into,*

> *such as the clerical profession and teaching, and to some extent in the legal profession, not to mention others, that the one large element which has done more to uplift them is the service in the Pullman Company* (Report of Commission of on Industrial Relations 1915, 9979 italics mine).

Lincoln attempts to justify the low wages paid to porters by emphasizing the generosity of the Pullman Company in giving Black men a job to begin with.

However, this did not mean that Lincoln embraced the idea of additional "racial uplifting" to place Blacks on the same social level as Whites. In the next sentence, Lincoln argues *against* the suggestion that wages should be raised for porters above $27.50, saying

> if you increase their wages without in some way stopping their tips, you simply make a larger income for them, and the question is whether that is desirable to do. . .you might easily soon have them earning more than skilled labor. (Report of Commission of on Industrial Relations 1915, 9992)

This raises the question, why would Lincoln consider it undesirable for porters to earn more than skilled labor (read: White men)? Probably because if Black men began earning more than White men, the logic of White supremacy, which supported the racialization of the porter job, would be seriously undermined. Also, if Lincoln was so interested in the "racial uplift" of Blacks—why would he be concerned with them earning higher incomes? He could have simply stated that they did not want to raise porters' wages for economic reasons. But he did not provide this purely economistic rationale.

It is always extremely difficult to make an argument by absence, to focus on what was *not* discussed, but given the dominant academic literature on racialized employment structures, it is striking that at no time in Hungerford's and Lincoln's testimony did they attribute the marginalization of Black workers to White workers' actions or the public's demands.

Additionally, no such evidence exists in the company executive committee minutes, internal correspondence between company executives, stockholder meeting minutes, and various other data from the Office of the President (01/01/01), the Office of the Vice President (01/01/02), Office of the Secretary and Treasurer (02/01/01), the Operating Department "Organizations (Labor Unions, Agreements, etc.)" (05/01/02), or the Pullman News (Pullman archive—HD8039 R1 P85). The absence of such instances is the more striking given the abundant evidence of the employer's own racial ideology, their sense that it was right and fitting for porters to be Black men, and their active promotion of the special qualities of Black men as singularly appropriate to the porter job.

"Minstrel Executives/Managers"

The Blackface minstrel show dedicated itself to reflecting and constructing racial boundaries between African Americans and Whites. Dating back to the 1830s, minstrel shows were an "instrument to the uses of White supremacy" (Saxton 1975, 27). Although the characters and songs differed, several consistent themes emerged across these minstrel acts. Unquestionably, the stereotype's key characteristics are the Black person's irresponsibility, childlike innocence, and never-ending good humor. These are a recurring subject in the minstrel show. The minstrel enjoys both his work and leisure activities; his worries are brief and fleeting. The simplicity and carelessness of the Black character indicate the necessity of strict direction and control by a White person. It is obvious that he is satisfied because of his delight with his lot. There is nothing to be feared or mistrusted about this joyful, guileless, and humorous creature, especially since he only demonstrates great dedication and loyalty to his White superiors (Dorman 1969).

Blackface minstrelsy reinforced alleged inherent, essential, and fundamental differences between the races. These shows also served to legitimize and naturalize existing racial discrimination. Not only are African Americans supposed to be at the bottom of the social ladder, they are happy to be there! If they are happy to be slaves, then how can one argue that the institution of slavery is bad? Even after slavery, Blackface minstrelsy would continue to reify racial differences and legitimize discrimination against Blacks.

The widespread image of Black men depicted in Blackface minstrel performances was especially compatible with Pullman's racialization of the porter as the happy, harmless, contented servant in need of a White man's supervision. Furthermore, the Pullman company glowingly publicized its White workers practice of minstrelsy and "Blackface" to caricature porters. In the June 1922 edition of the Pullman News, a full-page article celebrating White Pullman worker's minstrel acts under the caption "Famous Pullman Minstrels Successfully Sail the Seas." The famous Pullman Minstrels became able seamen this year and sailed "Beyond the Three-Mile Limit" to the delight of two audiences that packed the State theater on the evenings of May 10 and 11 while 1,000 others clamored vainly for tickets. "*President E.F. Carry of the Pullman Company was so pleased with it he dispatched the minstrels to the Michigan City Plant on May 27, where they entertained the H & B Social Club*" (Pullman News, June 1922 italics mine).

Not only did the Pullman company support its White workers performing Blackface minstrelsy, but the president of the company also actually encouraged the spread of these negative depictions of Black people. Numerous examples exist where the company paper displays images of its White workers and company executives performing in minstrel shows and appearing at company costume events in Blackface (see figure 3.4).

Figure 3.4 Behold Porter J. Henry Smith. *Source*: Pullman News February, 1925. Courtesy Newberry Library.

The accompanying text to this image reads:

> Sales Manager J. Henry Smith of the Auto Body Department of the Pullman Car & Manufacturing Corporation yearned to again re-enter the employ of the Pullman Company. So, for one night in December, he changed his color as he shifted employment and became a porter, and here you see him rendering courteous service to Mrs. Smith and saying it with a smile. All of this was a masked ball given at the Opera Club, Chicago. (Pullman News, February 1925)

In later years, the company would continue to promote performances by the Famous Pullman minstrels and show company managers in Blackface at company functions. This begs the question: Why did the Pullman Company decide to promote and disseminate Blackface minstrelsy? Once again, there was no particular reason why the company needed to engage in such racialization in the company newspaper. It is reasonable to assume this reflects the company executives' own racial ideology and their attempts to legitimize the racialized hierarchy they created on Pullman trains. Another theme that emerges in public discourse was an emphasis on the innate musical and entertainment capacities of porters.

A "Singing Race"—Happy to Entertain You!

The very first mention of porters in the Pullman News heralds the company's decision to sponsor a porters' musical chorus. This porters' musical chorus was created to entertain passengers, perform at company events, and travel the country promoting Pullman service. The company's publicly espoused reasoning clearly demonstrates the overt racialization of porters (Blacks) as inherently different from Whites. On the third page of the inaugural Pullman News edition in May 1922, the company announces the creation of a porters' musical chorus with a one-page article under the caption "Sponsors National Pullman Porters' Chorus: Company Engages Leading Musician to Instruct Its Men in Singing Folk Lore Melodies." The article describes the company's rationale:

> A movement of great importance to musical America has been sponsored by the Pullman Company. It has begun the organization of the Pullman Porters' Chorus. they represent a race whose emotions largely have been expressed in song. The Pullman Company has a twofold object in backing this musical enterprise. In the first place it believes musical education will be a good thing for the men. *They are of a singing race and music adds to their cheerfulness and contentment.* In the second place, it is believed a real service will be performed in developing and preserving the melodies of the American Negro (italics mine).

Pullman's executives and decision-makers operated from an essentialist view of race, which posits that there are fixed, predetermined, and immutable differences among human beings across racial categories. There is a sense of noblesse oblige in preserving musical traditions. The chorus won Pullman praise and publicity, as *Pullman News* reported in subsequent issues, noting some of the glowing editorials on the porters' chorus from various newspapers around the country. This depiction of Black men as happy entertainers served to legitimize customers' demands that porters entertain them on demand, a point confirmed by oral histories with porters (Perata 1996). The company continually sponsored and publicized the porters' chorus in later years.

"Racialized Jokes"

Jokes were another way in which the Pullman Company demonstrated the notion that Black and White people are inherently different. Racialized jokes were a part of the *Pullman News* from its inaugural edition. Between 1922 and 1925, the paper published over thirty jokes that explicitly mocked southern African Americans in a section titled "ATLANTA MONTHLY STORY." During this time period, only two other racial-ethnic jokes were published that applied to non-Blacks. A sampling of some of these jokes published every month in the company newspaper is as follows:

> The judge was new and somewhat irascible. The scene was laid in a courthouse down south. "You there," shouted the judge pointing to the old negro in front of him, "Are you the defendant?"
>
> "No, yer honor, I ain't," said the negro. "I ain't done nothing to be called names like that. I've got a lawyer to do the defending."
>
> "Then who are you?" demanded the honor.
> "I'se de gen'lman dat stole de chickens," was the reply
> (Pullman News, May 1923)
>
> "The manner in which a veteran porter can successfully handle fretful passengers was brought to the attention of Miss Julia Harpman, one of the star writers of the "New York Daily News," who in domestic life is Mrs. Westbrook Pegler, during a recent journey from Atlanta to New York. One woman, who alighted at Washington, was particularly hard to please, and Mrs. Pegler having been impressed with the courtesy and ability of the porter spoke to him of the departed one.
>
> "Yassum," she said "Ah didn't treat her submissive enough," he replied, "but, ma'am, Ah allus tries to obsequiate mahself, and didn' Ah treat yo' all submissive?"
>
> Mrs. Pegler agrees that he did, and also that he served breakfast to the kicker in her berth and carefully looked after her comfort."
> (Pullman News, November 1924)

It should be noted that Blacks were not the only subject of jokes in the company newspaper. On two occasions, persons of Scottish and Irish ancestry were also stereotyped.

> "A Car Works official of Scotch ancestry recently found it necessary to notify his wife that he would not be home that evening. The only definite point of time he could give her was six o'clock in the morning, he saying:
>
> "I'll ring you at 6 o'clock in the morning. When you hear the bell ring you'll know it will be me. Don't answer it and I'll get my nickel back."

The same official recently returned home from a trip to the other side. He visited one particular spot where it's the custom to throw a penny across an arm of water. He was asked as to his prowess in this direction and responded:

> "I almost lost the penny! The string broke!"
> (Pullman News, November 1924)

The important difference is that these views of Scottish and Irish people did not prevent individuals from this background from ascending to positions of authority. In fact, President E. F. Carry was of Irish descent and openly contributed to Irish causes.

Why would a company run such jokes in its official newspaper? There was plenty of other material within each edition so it is hard to argue that the jokes were included merely as filler. It is reasonable to conclude that such jokes served to reinforce racial group differences and in the case of Black workers to justify their position at the bottom of the Pullman workplace hierarchy. Notably such jokes targeting Blacks ceased to be published in the Pullman News after the Brotherhood of Sleeping Car Porters was organized in 1925.

Although porters secured a victory in that Black people were no longer the target of such jokes, they were not successful in eliminating the company's support for minstrel shows and Blackface.

Feminizing the Porter Job

Another way in which porters were denied the "manhood" afforded to conductors was through the feminization of their labor. Paid and unpaid childcare and other forms of reproductive labor (such as cooking and cleaning) have historically been conceptualized as women's work. This work is usually rendered invisible (Daniels 1987), and its performance creates dominant and subordinate relations between men and women (Hartmann 1981). Feminized labor, such as childcare, remains largely defined in contrast to "real work." Also, women of color have been overrepresented as servants, performing the laborious tasks of maintaining the home while their White employers served as housewives and hostesses. As reproductive tasks have been increasingly removed from the household and performed within publicly organized institutions, racial-ethnic women have continued to perform the "back-room" work (e.g., hospital cafeteria workers), while White women maintain more public and supervisory roles (e.g., nurses). This race-gender division of reproductive labor reproduces racialized practices of subordination and racial inequality (Duffy 2007; Glenn 2002; Rollins 1985).

In this case, racial patterns commonly associated with women of color and servitude are replicated with Black men on Pullman trains. Porters were required to perform labor commonly associated with women—making beds, serving food, cleaning up after others, and being deferential. Pullman also feminized the porter job to the extent that Black men are portrayed as being appropriate childcare providers. On numerous occasions, porters were described and depicted caring for White children with a smile on their face.A few occurrences of many the Pullman company publicized linking Black men to caring for White children can be seen in figures 3.5 and 3.6 .

The caption mentions Porter "Joe" Glasgow "with his little friends, most of whom he cares for on his Pere Marquette Line." (See figure 3.7.)

PULLMAN NEWS 225

Generations Know 'Joe' Glasgow

FOR 20 years Porter "Joe" Glasgow of Chicago Central Dist. has run on the "Resort Special," the Pere Marquette's famous train from Chicago to Lake Michigan east coast summer refuges, patronized by Chicago and St. Louis people in particular. During that time he has handled several generations of Pullman passengers and been a family retainer to all. Youngsters whom he has carried in his arms have, in time, turned over their children to him for attention and, as he is but 48, he is likely to be the friend and counselor for at least another generation, in the ordinary course of events. As the *Traverse City (Mich.) Record-Eagle* put it in a recent story:

"'Joe' has his regular customers, just as a grocer, a physician or a bootlegger has his, and when they come within the realm of 'Joe's' service they place themselves utterly in his hands. 'Joe' knows what station furnishes the best milk for babies, which dress to keep out of the bag at night to best meet the temperatures at the next

Figure 3.5 Porter Glasgow Carries White Toddler. *Source*: Pullman News April, 1926. Courtesy Newberry Library.

Figure 3.6 Porter Glasgow in Juvenile Parade. *Source*: Pullman News, June 1927. Courtesy Newberry Library.

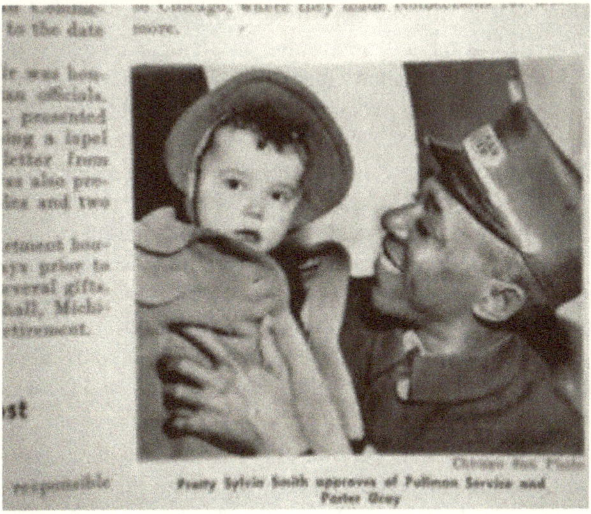

Figure 3.7 Porter with White Baby. *Source*: Pullman News, December 1928. Courtesy Newberry Library.

This case contributes to the literature on reproductive labor and race-gender inequality by illustrating that similar hierarchical patterns were replicated in the porter job. Social practices most commonly associated with hierarchical relationships between class-privileged White women and women of color appear between conductors and porters. The conductor was responsible for the quality of service provided on the train (akin to hosting a dinner party), while the porter was compelled to provide the actual labor, which made "Pullman service" desirable.

The extent to which the porter job was publicly feminized and linked to childcare provision on Pullman trains was one more mechanism that denied porters the "manhood" status afforded to the conductor.

Race in Private Discourse between Company Executives

This section examines the internal correspondence between Pullman Company executives regarding race. Specifically, racial discourse recorded in employee disciplinary files, private internal correspondence between company executives, and official company responses to private requests for data regarding racialized work is analyzed.

The higher wages paid to conductors are not a reflection of effort expended by workers. Internal correspondence between company executives illustrates that the company believed conductors did not work hard.

> While the conductor is on duty an average of 9 hours a day, he is not actually working or performing any labor, either mental or physical, during more than fifty percent of that time, on average. Some considerable portion of his time, perhaps one hour during each day, is spent either in the station or at the car awaiting the arrival or passengers and checking them in as they do arrive . . . After the train has started and the conductor and porters have their passengers located, and the conductor has made his collections, the major portion of his work for the entire trip is finished . . . there are long periods between station stops during which the conductor has no work whatsoever to perform, and can either devote his time to reading magazines or newspapers or to conversation with his passengers, as may suit his fancy—Feb. 10, 1920 From Office of Supervisor of Industrial Relations. (F.L Simmons (06/01/01) Box 1).

This acknowledgment that conductors were afforded down-time to read newspapers and lounge is particularly striking given the fact that porters were routinely cautioned in their disciplinary files for reading newspapers or being overly talkative with passengers. Additionally, a good conductor should possess the ability to command obedience from subordinates.

Evaluation forms for porter trainees provide important insight into the racialized ideology underlying the racialized hierarchy on Pullman trains in

1928. These forms were titled "Certificate of Instructions for New Employees" and were created by the Employee and Labor Relations Department of the Pullman company. Qualities desired in a porter include "Attentive, Industrious, Obedient, Patient, Quiet." Qualities not desired include "Insubordinate and Talkative" (06/02/02, Box 8/Folder 117). In addition to these qualities, porters were responsible for an inordinate amount of work.

A 1914 circular addressed to porters entitled "Things to Do" contains the following directives regarding being a good porter:

> "Always wear clean linen."
>
> "Have your uniform cleaned and pressed up." "Keep your shoes polished."
>
> "Black passengers' shoes."
>
> "Dust passengers' clothing, asking them to step aside."
>
> "Call out stations when trains enter terminal stations or on route." "Tender pillows to passengers."
>
> "Tender hat bags to lady passengers." "Keep washstands cleaned up."
>
> "Keep cuspidors cleaned up."
>
> "Keep your lockers cleaned up, clean papers on the shelves." "Keep clean jackets with full set of buttons."
>
> "Have lanterns lighted at night and in position for immediate use." "Keep soiled linen picked up."
>
> "Keep plenty of clean towels in the racks." "Keep whisk brooms in the toilet room."
>
> "Fasten all berth safety cords."
>
> "Light your night lamps when other lights are lighted." "Answer bells promptly."
>
> "Courtesy is the best thing you can give passengers and have in stock. It costs you the least and gives best results."
>
> "Wipe window sills often." "Guard cars closely."
>
> "Assist passengers with ladders when getting in and out of upper berths." " Make up berths promptly at night."
>
> "Be out at all stations where trains stop to receive passengers and assist with the baggage."
>
> "Properly regulate ventilation."
>
> "Look closely after the regulation of the Garland ventilators, those marked 'V' to be opened, or part of them closed, as the weather will indicate."
>
> "Temperature of your cars should be regulated by steam in the winter months, to be introduced through the inlet valve in the heater room."
>
> "Keep combs and brushes clean."
>
> "Turn out the lights promptly after passengers have retired."

"Have an equipment box supplied at all times at home station." "Keep uniform coats buttoned while on duty."

"Read station order books, sign them, and be sure you understand the orders and comply with them. If not understood, call at the office for an explanation." "Render all assistance possible to lady passengers and children, especially old ladies and men and sick passengers."

"Wire vacancies according to local instructions."

"Use camp stool at the end of aisle at night to guard cars."

"Pull down all window shades at night when starting to make down berths." "Wipe deflectors and screens before placing them in windows and lockers."

(1915 Pullman Congressional Testimony Transcripts, evidence introduced by Chairman Walsh)

Porters were expected to perform all these tasks for significantly lower wages than conductors. The list is also significant, however, in that it enumerates a long list of specific physical tasks; the wide range of actions that needed to be taken makes it all the more remarkable that the Pullman company and its executives so emphasized demeanor and subservience.

They Should Know Their Place!

It is worth noting that company executives were conscientious about making sure porters "knew their place." Racial ideology is so hegemonic that it rarely warrants overt articulation. However, when examining internal Pullman memoranda between company executives, it became clear that during moments of contestation, racial ideology was expressed more overtly. Rare examples focused on porters not "knowing their place." In 1927, a district superintendent sent a memo to Pullman Company president E. F. Carry, an Irish American who started as a conductor. The correspondence below is in regard to a porter who was challenging his termination from the Pullman Company and the justification for why the decision was made to bar him from any future employment with the company:

CONFIDENTIAL MEMORANDUM FOR MR. E.F. CARRY, PRESIDENT

This porter was discharged because of his insubordinate attitude when questioned about his controversy with a Conductor. This porter has had three hearings and in each case his petition for reinstatement has been denied, and in view of his actions and attitude the decisions could not properly be otherwise.

This ex-porter *has the characteristics of a West Indian* and it is generally believed by the conductors and porters in the New Orleans District that he is a West Indian, although he claims Canada as his birth place.

He seems unable to accept instructions from a conductor without showing resentment and insubordination.

He was terminated by the district superintendent because he refused to sign a prepared statement which I quote below.

> I understand that the Pullman conductors have jurisdiction over all other car employees on cars . . . I admit that the conductor had the right to question me about the preparation of beds on my car and promise that hereafter I will answer questions of conductors in a respectful way I thoroughly understand that if in the future I refuse to accept the authority of my conductor or obey his instructions, I will be subject to dismissal.

The porter absolutely refused to sign the statement. This porter has been in the service for about four years, was a good porter so far as the performance of his duties was concerned, and got along with his passengers fairly well, *but is of the West Indian type; very independent; thinks he is as good as any conductor*. Not to be re-employed (Pullman Archive 06/01/01 Box 2, Folder 34. Italics mine).

This memo demonstrates that performing the required tasks was not all porters were expected to do. Company executives wanted porters who "knew their place"—namely, they were supposed to accept that they were "not as good as any White man."

In later years, the company would be more specific regarding which groups of workers were undesirable. A 1941 confidential correspondence titled "Memorandum on Features to be Considered in the Employment of New Porters" sent by the personnel director to all district superintendents details which types of Black men company executives felt were suited and unsuited to be servants.

> "It is considered proper that applicants complete grammar school education and preferably some high school. Men who have attended colleges or universities are not considered the most desirable material to act as servants; therefore, care must be taken in considering them.
>
> The sheik type do not make good servants and should not be considered. Do not employ a light-complexioned man. *West Indians are not to be considered.*"
>
> (Files of G.H. Gibney (Personnel Director Correspondence with District Superintendents 04/02/03.)

The ideal porter had no college experience and was supposed to be dark-skinned. Presumably, a light-skinned or college-educated Black man could not be relied upon to remember his position at the bottom of the racial hierarchy. The undesirability of West Indians was repeated in internal correspondence, begging the question, Why was this the case?

By 1924, U.S. residents of West Indian descent numbered more than 300,000. Many became active in the public sphere of their new home. Their importance lay not only in their numbers but in their concentration and contributions. Many moved to New York City and played a vital role in Harlem's "New Negro" movement. Historian Winston James (1998) has demonstrated that West Indians "held aloft the banner of Ethiopia," advocating Black unity and racial uplift. He also argues that

> The Caribbean presence in radical[ism] in the U.S. was remarkable in . . . three important respects. First, it was out of proportion to the group's numerical weight within the Black population. Second, Caribbeans founded and led not only Black nationalist [groups] like the UNIA, but also important political currents on the revolutionary socialist left. Third, the migrants also provided some of the most distinguished Black intellectuals at the time. (184)

West Indians such as Marcus Garvey, C. L. R. James, Claude McKay, and Claudia Jones advocated for "Black consciousness" and helped to set the political agenda for Black America (Watkins-Owens 1996).

Given the prominence of West Indians in the movement for Black racial equality, it is not surprising that they would be associated with radicalism and challenging the position of Blacks within a racist society. The image of the race-conscious West Indian was antithetical to the ideal type of porter (a southern Black man who knows his place) the Pullman Company was looking for. Unlike his West Indian counterpart, the ideal porter was from the southern United States and had accepted the taken-for-granted racial hierarchies. The Pullman Company's stated aversion to hiring West Indians and the reasons why demonstrate that company executives' racial views about different "types" of Black men became nuanced over time. What remains the same over time is that their racial discourse still privileges southern-born Black men as ideal porters. It is striking that this would remain the case even though, regardless of skin color or nationality, porters would be paid the same wage. Apparently, southern Black men were preferable because they were viewed as more pliable labor and, specifically, because company executives believed they made "better servants." By definition, an ideal servant recognizes their place in the social order—obviously, "race-conscious" men could not be trusted to conform to the rules of social interaction between unequal parties.

This chapter focused on employers' racialized discourse because it provides insight into how employers' beliefs about African Americans contributed to these workers' relegation to inferior jobs.

> Racism is dialectical. Racist structure is legitimated by racist ideology. Actors are schooled within this context so that differential treatment of people of color becomes normalized, expected, and part of everyday practice. At the micro

> level, actors themselves buy into the racist structure and act in ways that perpetuate it. Racism is hegemonic so that it often appears invisible. Participating in racist practices—knowingly or unknowingly—reinforces the hierarchies of racism by taking the rules for granted. (Myers and Williamson 2001, 5)

By analyzing both public and private discourse, one cannot identify whether or not public racialization reflects employers appeasing White workers or the White public. However, the private discourse *does* explicitly demonstrate that White management believed the porter job as suited for a Black man who "knows his place." The entirely White male Pullman company executives were motivated by profit-making motives, gender ideology, and racial group interests. An attempt to disentangle which factors (profit, race-gender ideology) contributed to the marginalization of Black workers on the train is not necessarily feasible since they are interconnected, as Du Bois articulates in *Darkwater.*

This chapter examined the ways that company executives reproduced racist structure and ideology through their racialized discourse in public and private spaces. Racialized discourse normalizes and legitimizes racist attitudes and practices. According to Feagin (2020), "an ideology is a set of principles and views that embodies the basic interests of a particular social group" (69). Therefore, analyzing racialized discourse is an important tool to understand the perpetuation of racism within a hierarchical structure.

Furthermore, because attitudes affect behavior (Feagin 2020), examining racial discourse is key to understanding the legitimation of continued discrimination against Blacks in the Pullman company. Analyses of racist discourse provide a link between people's discriminatory actions and the structure of racial inequality within an organization. This chapter specifically focused on the ways in which the Pullman company engaged in racialized discourse to normalize company executives' decision to hire Black men as porters and White men as conductors.

Taken alone, one might be able to argue that certain data might not necessarily reflect racist ideology. However, the totality of the data, seen in conjunction with employers' maintenance of strict racial boundaries in the conductor and porter jobs, I argue, demonstrates a pattern of employers racializing southern Blacks as different, inferior, and appropriate for service. Unless one is willing to accept that Pullman company executives somehow escaped socialization into a racist society—it is, at the very least, plausible to assume that they shared some of these views. Furthermore, since company executives attached racial meanings to the conductor and porter jobs and used various types of discourse to explain and legitimize this practice—one must at least take seriously the argument that such racial ideology negatively contributed to Black workers' job prospects. This racialized discourse and practice of marginalizing Black workers reflected *both* employers' existing beliefs *and* served to legitimize their profit-making motives. The counter-argument (employers were not racist but merely responding to racist White workers and/or passenger demands) is hard to support given what company executives said to themselves privately.

The gradual shift from mass transit aboard trains to airplanes began in the late 1920s. What happens when service work moves from the railroad to the skies? Would employers in the airline industry keep the practice of hiring cheap Black male labor? What stories would be told to justify a new system of workplace hierarchy? These questions are the focus of the following chapter.

Chapter 4

White Femininity Takes Flight, 1910s–1970s

This chapter discusses the emergence of the airline industry and the first wave of male and female aviators from 1910 to 1930. We examine employers' role between 1930 and 1970 in solidifying the association between masculinity and flying. Next, we focus on the first service workers aboard airplanes. In this instance, airline executives create and explicitly feminize the flight attendant position. Attention is paid to the job requirements and training employers made necessary for the stewardess position. During the 1930s and 1960s, the role of a flight attendant broke, constructed, and reinforced race-gender norms about White femininity.

THE TRANSITION FROM TRAINS TO AIRPLANES

At the start of the twentieth century, railroads were Americans' primary means of intercity travel. The shift from commercial passenger railroad travel to flying for long-distance journeys at the turn of the twentieth century was slow. Train travel accounted for 98 percent of all intertown passenger travel in 1916. In 1929, the railroad industry accounted for 30 billion passenger miles, compared to a meager 30 million passenger miles for airlines (Omelia and Waldock 2003, 24). As late as 1939, airlines accounted for only 2 percent of passenger miles. It would take until the mid-1950s for airlines to overtake trains in passenger traffic (Rust 2012, 158).

In the early 1900s, airplanes were an unknown novelty to most people. It is estimated that only one in a thousand Americans had ever seen an aircraft in 1910. Competitive air meetings provided the only opportunity for people to view the awe-inspiring sight of humans in flight. In 1911, while attending a competitive air meeting in Los Angeles, newspaper titan William Randolph

Hearst was inspired to offer a $50,000 prize for the first person to fly an airplane cross-country *within thirty days.* During this era, air travel was not a plausible rival to the transcontinental railroad, which took approximately *eight days.* Former race-car driver Cal Rogers ultimately claimed the prize and garnered significant fanfare in the popular press. However, air travel was framed as a sensational spectacle, not a practical means of transporting Americans from place to place (Rust 2012, 5). Even though aviation garnered considerable public enthusiasm, it still needed to be viewed as a viable mode of transportation. The federal government would play a pivotal role in getting Americans airborne.

Role of the Federal Government

The federal government's interventions and subsidies would prove necessary to establish the passenger transport aviation industry. Dating back to the stagecoach era in the 1850s, the federal government played a role in subsidizing private commercial passenger transport enterprises (Rust 2012, 10). The federal government also funded the construction of the transcontinental railroads linking the East and West coasts. These public investments made the creation and profitability of privately-owned railroad businesses possible; the same would be true for aviation companies. Historically, the U.S. government has been a primary source of funding for improvements to communication and transportation. Meaning taxpayers have continually subsidized capitalists. In the nineteenth century, scores of companies received 131 million acres of land—approximately 7 percent of the country's total area—and millions of dollars in subsidies to build a railroad network linking the country with rails of steel. Aviation was no exception to this trend. There was no way for private enterprises to construct a canal or rail system during the nineteenth century without governmental assistance, as the financial returns on private investments would not materialize for many years. In the early twentieth century, few financiers considered aviation a worthwhile investment (Rust 2012, 22).

Transporting mail would provide the impetus for direct government intervention in the aviation industry. The first official airmail flight took place on September 25, 1911. Aviators such as Earl Ovington and Katherine Stinson transported letters in the following years. In the spring of 1918, the U.S. Congress appropriated $100,000 for the first regularly scheduled airmail service. Hired for this task were U.S. Army pilots, thereby excluding women from the job. From its inception, the U.S. postal service hoped its airmail service would lay the foundation for civil aviation in the United States. In the early years, planes only flew during daylight, meaning cross-country mail took seventy-eight hours to arrive. The advent of lighting and flares on planes and lit landing strips on the ground would make air travel much more efficient—creating the transcontinental air system. These inventions meant that by 1924, it only took thirty-five hours of flying around the clock to deliver mail coast-to-coast. These speeds eclipsed those of the trains and subsequently cost privately-owned railroad businesses lost revenues, "particularly from banks using airmail to shorten the float time of checks from coast to coast" (Rust 2012, 24). A well-known supporter of railroad company interests, U.S. representative M. Clyde Kelly, introduced the Contract Air Mail Act of 1925. The Act was approved by Congress with little debate and created a system where private contractors would carry airmail, with mail payment acting as a subsidy (Rust 2012, 24). The Post Office gave contracts to businesses to deliver mail utilizing the taxpayer-funded transcontinental air system. The awarding of these contracts provided the impetus for several new enterprises. In fact, "most U.S. major airlines would eventually claim lineage to one or more of the companies that operated the first 12 contract airmail routes" (Rust 2012, 24).

From Transporting Mail to Serving Passengers

At its inception, transporting passengers took a back seat to mail delivery. These companies were created to service airmail and were paid by the Post Office for the amount of mail they carried. There was no strong market for passenger air travel outside of daredevils and air enthusiasts. Unlike railroad stations, airports were inconveniently located outside of the city center. The flight cost significantly more than rail travel. In the early 1930s, flying cross-country cost between $260 and $440. On a train, the exact trip cost as little as $64 (Vantoch 2013, 12). Flying was bumpy and could not rival the comforts and service provided on a Pullman train. On a train, passengers could get five-course meals, visit the smoking/game car, call upon a porter to shine their shoes or bring them a beverage whenever desired, and sleep in a private berth. In the 1920s, air travelers were lucky to receive a cold lunch box and bottle of coffee handed to them by the copilot. Despite its discomforts, there was a growing market among business travelers who valued the speed of travel. Business executives such as C. R. Borkland of *Popular Aviation* magazine argued that flying was ultimately cheaper and more productive.

> Figure the expense of berths, meals, tips, and all the other little extras you never can remember . . . Then put a conservative value on your wasted time, the time you spend reading magazines on the train, looking out the window, trying to sleep nights, trying to stay awake daytimes so you can sleep nights. (as quoted in Rust 2012, 40)

Borkland and others in the aviation industry argued that journeys by air were the future of business travel. However, the airline experience would need significant improvement and better marketing if it wanted to lure business professionals away from the luxuries of a Pullman train.

In 1927, the publicity around Charles Lindbergh's nonstop flight from New York to Paris allowed business leaders to market air travel to the American masses. Between 1927 and 1929, eager investors purchased $400 million in aviation securities (Rust 2012, 43). This influx of capital into aviation enterprises helped spur the transformation to commercial passenger air travel, which began in the 1930s. Established in 1929, Transcontinental Air Transport (TAT) was one of the businesses that emerged in this era. Using a combination of air and rail travel, TAT could transport passengers across the country in *forty-eight hours,* half the time it took on the fastest cross-country train. With noted White supremacist Charles Lindbergh as its figurehead, TAT was a trailblazer. Lindbergh, along with Clement M. Keys and other financiers, sought to forge ties with railroad companies and launched the business as a joint air-rail operation. Combining air and rail made sense. Airlines followed railroad tracks for navigation between the two coasts and could stop at cities along the way where railroads already had stations. Ultimately, two established rail companies joined with Lindbergh and his financiers to establish the TAT company. The creation of TAT was viewed by the general public as the railroad leaping into the sky as a result of its extensive involvement in the project.

Promotional literature of the time emphasized that TAT's passengers could sleep well during the night aboard the finest raid accommodations and soar during the day on the wings of flying Pullmans, "it was a clear case of 'railroads sprouting wings'" (Rust 2012, 44). Other companies entered the airline business. In the early 1930s, following several bankruptcies and mergers, four major domestic airlines emerged—United, American, Eastern, and TWA. After a rocky start, commercial passenger air travel was beginning to grow. By 1933, over half a million passengers were transported on the four major domestic airlines (Vantoch 2013, 13).

This newly emerging airline industry would ban women from piloting. Although it would appear "natural" that only men would be pilots, the history of women in flight demonstrates that the subsequent link between masculinity and flying was not by any means inevitable.

Lady Pilots: Breaking, Then Reinforcing Race-Gender Norms (1910s–1930s)

In the 1920s, women played an important role in the early aviation industry, and the presence of female pilots reflected new gender norms about White womanhood. The dominant gender stereotypes of the time still revolved around the "cult of true womanhood." Most White women were still expected to be demure, submissive, and domesticated. However, women had recently won suffrage, and popular culture was filled with images of the "flapper." This new strand of White femininity was depicted as independent, capable, and willing to challenge gender norms. Women in flight were reflective of this new version of femininity associated with White women. The public was regularly regaled with the exploits of Amelia Earhart, Jacqueline Cochran, Ruth Nichols, and other "lady pilots." Their flights were widely covered in the national media, and some women could earn significant income through air-race sponsorships and teaching others how to fly.

> Women aviators could work as "barnstormers"—stunt pilots who traveled across the country performing treacherous aerial feats such as plane-to-plane transfers via hanging rope ladders. The illustrious Ruth Law, a particularly successful female aviator, for example, earned $9,000 per week performing airborne stunts. Law's tour de force: climbing out of the cockpit onto the wing.

Bessie Coleman (see figure 4.1) was another prominent "lady pilot." She was a Black woman from Chicago who received her license from the

Figure 4.1 Bessie Coleman, Aviatrix. *Source*: Schomburg Center for Research in Black Culture, Jean Blackwell Hutson Research and Reference Division, The New York Public Library. (1925). Bessie Coleman, aviatrix; Snapped in Berlin, Germany. Retrieved from https://digitalcollections.nypl.org/items/510d47de-5184-a3d9-e040-e00a18064a99.

Federation Aeronautique Internationale in Paris and became the first Black woman in the world to have an international pilot's license. Bessie Coleman returned to the United States in 1921 and became a media sensation. The public called her "Queen Bess," and she was one of the most famous stunt pilots in the country. Audiences were happy to pay to watch her perform at places such as the Checkerboard Airdome, now known as Chicago's Midway Airport. There, she performed daredevil stunts that dazzled the audience (Creasman 1997). Women pilots would go on to found their own organizations, such as the Ninety-Nines, to expand aviation opportunities for other women. In addition to carving out spaces for themselves, female aviators also received support from the airline industry itself, at least initially.

Business executives who were eager to transform the public's impression of flying looked toward White women for a public image makeover for the airline industry. While flying was widely celebrated and glamorized in popular culture, it was also dangerous. During World War I, newspapers were filled with accounts of courageous, daredevil pilots. The subsequent popularity of air show competitions only reinforced the idea that taking to the air was for adventurous adrenaline junkies. However, widespread news coverage of airplane accidents and fatalities fed the public perception that flying in an airplane was a risky endeavor. Like their predecessors in the automobile industry, airline executives decided to utilize women to prove that their mode of conveyance was indeed safe.

Women played a significant role in improving aviation's image. To counter the dangerous image of flying and make flying seem safer to the public, aviation companies sponsored races, record-breaking flights, and other special events featuring female pilots. In the early days of car promotion, this strategy mimicked automotive publicity events. Car manufacturers sponsored women in the 1910s to drive across the country to reassure the public that cars were easy and safe; similarly, airline officials used women pilots to prove that flying was safe and easy (Vantoch 2013, 12).

For a brief moment in the 1920s, business executives utilized the shifting ideologies reflected in the "flapper" to embrace women taking on new public roles that would previously have been reserved for men. The industry's embrace of women pilots would soon fade.

Furthermore, although Amelia Earhart and others gained notoriety in the 1920s as female pilots, they were still viewed as novelties in an ostensibly masculine endeavor (Whitelegg 2007, 33).

Kicking Women Out of the Cockpit

By the 1930s, employers in the aviation industry had firmly decided to shut women out of the cockpit. Employers at a domestic U.S. airline didn't hire a female pilot until 1973, when Frontier Airlines hired Emily Warner as a copilot (Douglas 2004). The executive's decision to exclude women from piloting would reinforce the ostensibly "natural" link between masculinity and flying airplanes. Additionally, White men's exclusion of women from pilot unions and their engagement in "social closure" and "opportunity hoarding," along with employers' hiring decisions, conspired to shut women out of the domestic airline piloting profession. For example, when Central Airlines hired Helen Richey in 1934 as a short-term publicity stunt, the all-male pilots' union complained to airline management and to the Air Commerce Department that Richey was physically too weak to fly in bad weather. The department had previously considered grounding all female pilots during their menstrual periods, and it backed the male pilots' association by making women pilots only fly in good weather (Vantoch 2013). Clearly, a group of male pilots and aviation regulators were working in tandem to assert that the female body was, by definition, unsuited for the role of pilot. Women would be shut out of the profession of commercial piloting for four decades. Female pilots were battling the invocation of the hegemony of White masculinity from both their employers and potential coworkers. This systematic exclusion of all women and non-Whites from piloting between the 1930s and 1970s served to make the publicly viewed connection between manhood and piloting even more intractable.

Many early pilots had previous military service, so on the surface, it makes sense that the pilot job was the exclusive domain of men in the commercial aviation industry. In this case, labor supply might appear to be the driving force behind this workplace segregation. Although it should be noted that aviators such as Katherine Stinson worked as airmail pilots for the Post Office. Many women were privately trained. Women in the 1910s to early 1930s had been encouraged by the aviation industry to compete in air show competitions and received sponsorships and widespread publicity. Furthermore, during World War II, women had flown in WASP. Lastly, "while precise data do not exist on how many stewardesses had previously trained as pilots, it was not uncommon for stewardesses hired during the 1930s, 1940s to have pilot licenses or at least some training flying planes" (Vantoch 2013, 223).

Popularly acclaimed pilots such as Charles Lindbergh were depicted as the embodiment of masculinity.

> Pilots were admired as virile figures who bravely rode the clouds "by the seat of their pants." By necessity and training, pilots had to withstand high-altitude conditions . . . that were wholly foreign to those who remained on the ground. Pilots needed faster reflexes and exceptional depth perception. Clearly, these men were extraordinary. (Rust 2012, 30)

In addition to their debonair outfits, early pilots on commercial flights also carried a sidearm gun in accordance with Post Office regulations. The combination of employers' discriminatory hiring practices and cultural symbolism ensured that by the early 1930s, the pilot job had become completely masculinized.

Onboard Airline Service Workers—Inventing the Flight Attendant

For several reasons, it would make sense for the service workers on the railroad to seamlessly transition their labor to an aircraft. Black men were the most recognizable public "transport servants," and Pullman porters were widely regarded as the epitome of luxury servitude. Also, many of the founders of the airline industry were also railroad executives and were familiar with the reputation Black men had garnered on the rails. Alternatively, they could have turned to Filipino men who were working as waiters and attendants on U.S. passenger ships. It is important to note that it was not self-evident that servitude in the air would be the domain of women, let alone White women. In Europe, young (White) men were utilized as the first air attendants. Women were introduced to the airline industry through happenstance. Much like the porters, it was not predestined that women would work as attendants in the air. Also akin to the porters, women would enter a workplace environment that employers had deliberately and consciously segregated along the lines of race and gender. The social identities of those assigned to certain job titles would go on to shape the very nature of the work. Furthermore, because these "public servant/hostess" positions were race-gender typed, it comes to seem as though workers are inherently performing the tasks their identity innately makes most suitable. A key tenet of sociology is that much of what we consider "naturally occurring" hierarchy is in fact the reflection of socializing forces such as media and even interactions with workers.

White Male Stewards

Early on, airlines were focused on delivering mail, and carrying passengers was an occasional benefit. These initial flights offered little to nothing in the way of in-flight service. The first official in-flight servants were "cabin boys" hired by Britain's Daimler Airways in 1922. Their duties were "to weigh and load passengers and mail, check passengers in, and in the late 1920s, to pass out boxed lunches of fried chicken" (Omelia and Waldock 2003, 9). Later in the decade, European airlines recruited these adult male "stewards" from "first-class hotels, restaurants, and ocean liners" (Barry 2007, 15). Within the United States, the first official flight attendants were introduced in 1926 by Stout Air Services. These White men were "aerial couriers" that served food and handled baggage. Other airlines would follow suit by hiring White male "couriers" to provide rudimentary in-flight service for a small number of passengers.

As in-flight service improved, young White men were still the only ones working aboard airplanes. For example, on TAT, "the sons of wealthy TAT investors, these young men brought the passenger to the airfield from a downtown collection point, delivered catered meals to the waiting airplanes, and handled baggage" (Rust 2012, 53). Their responsibilities included weighing luggage, storing bags, hanging passengers' coats, pointing out the lavatory, passing out magazines, and serving pre-made food and beverages on carts from a kitchenette in the back of the plane (Rust 2012, 54).

The service these stewards conducted was shielded from the aura of subservience (ala Porters) in two key ways, the abolition of tipping and pathways to executive work. Early airline executives decided to do away with tipping when it came to their White employees.

> Gratis service and racial "fellowship" eased the problem of White male subservience and encouraged a sense of exclusive community in the face of fear and far less comfort than Pullman cars. Airline management further diminished any servile connotations attached to stewards' work by treating it as a possible stepping-stone to positions as pilots or executives. (Barry 2007, 16–17)

Between 1926 and 1930, there was no reason to think that White men would not continue to be the ideal flight attendants. By the 1930s, opportunities for women to fly had diminished significantly as airline companies that had once utilized "lady pilots" to prove the safety of flying were now refusing to hire women pilots to transport mail or passengers (Vantoch 2013, 14). It also appeared that young White men were firmly cemented as the labor source for flight service. It would take the efforts of Ellen Church and an act of happenstance to create a space for women to work in the air.

White Femininity Takes Flight—The Role of Happenstance

Ellen Church was a twenty-six-year-old nurse who took flying classes at the local airport. While Church desperately wanted to be a pilot, she realized that by 1930, opportunities for women in aviation had narrowed considerably. Airline executives decided that women would not be hired as pilots in their industry (Whitelegg 2007, 35). In an attempt to secure women a place in the newly burgeoning airline industry, Church came up with the idea of hiring trained nurses (such as herself) to work as flight cabin attendants. She pitched the idea to Steve Stimpson, an executive at Boeing Air Transport (later United Airlines) in February 1930. Stimpson was already in the process of hiring White male attendants and wrote a memo to A. G. Kinsman stating that he had lined up good prospects and had interviewed some of them six times to confirm that they were "good men." However, that same day, apparently having just met with Church, Stimpson sent another memo to Kinsman proposing they utilize female attendants instead.

Stimpson's memo was clear on the specific type of woman he was now considering for the position; he would not hire "the flapper type of girl." He wanted women

> who had seen enough of men to not be inclined to chase them around the block at every opportunity . . . you know as well as I do, and you know that they are not given to flightiness—I mean in the head. The average graduate nurse is a girl with some horse sense and is very practical. (Vantoch 2013, 15)

Stimpson's attempt to introduce female attendants was initially resisted by his superiors, who did not see the value of diverging from the utilization of young White men for the task. But Stimpson pressed on by stressing the potential psychological benefits of hiring young women.

He telegrammed the following to Boeing executives:

> It strikes me that there would be a great psychological punch to having young women stewardesses . . . I have in mind a couple of graduate nurses that would make exceptional stewardesses. . . . Imagine the psychology of having young women as regular members of the crew. Imagine the national publicity we would get from it, and the tremendous effect it would have on the traveling public. Also, imagine the value they would be to us not only in the neater and nicer method of serving food bt looking out for the passenger's welfare. (Stimpson 1930)

In spite of his pleadings, Stimpson's bosses were still unconvinced and insisted on proceeding with the hiring of young men as originally planned. According to Vantoch, the wife and children of William Patterson, assistant to the president of Boeing (later became company president), helped save the day. Patterson was originally wedded to the idea of hiring young White men but his family, who had experienced bouts of air sickness, proclaimed they would much rather have a woman hold their hair back when vomiting than a man. Patterson subsequently signed off on a three-month trial for female flight attendants (Vantoch 2013, 15).

Recollecting the events years later in a speech, Stimpson asserted:

> I sent a long letter . . . telling him all the reasons for hiring stewardesses that I could think of; the psychology of having young women as regular members of

> the crew, the publicity it would bring us, the jobs they could do, such as keeping records, filing reports, issuing tickets, etc.
>
> I promptly got a telegram in reply—"No." It was the shortest telegram I have ever received. Then William A. Patterson, assistant to the company president, got in the act. He was pretty dubious about it too, but after talking it over with his wife Vera, he became convinced it might be worth a try. He gave me permission to hire eight stewardesses for a three-month trial period.
>
> We were off to a flying start in more ways than one. We had one month to hire and train the girls, design and have their uniforms made, write a manual, work out schedules, and many other things such as, even in those days, that of adequate expense accounts. (Stimpson 1955)

The airline's trial run would thus begin the seemingly "natural" link between flight attendants and womanhood. Men were not completely shut off from the flight attendant occupation. Pan Am, an international carrier, began using male stewards in 1928 and excluded women until 1944. However, by the early 1930s, the big four domestic carriers switched to women attendants. Although some airlines continued to employ a few male attendants, by the mid-1930s the occupation was heavily feminized (Vantoch 2013). This imagery of the female flight attendant became embedded within the popular culture of the era.

Although company executives decided to start by exclusively hiring young White men and had originally resisted the idea of hiring women to work as flight attendants, it would ultimately work to their economic benefit. It is crucial to note that employers did not begin with the idea of finding a cheaper labor force; they stumbled into it. It's interesting to note that employers didn't proceed as "rational" economic actors, merely concerned with finding the best worker available regardless of their identity. There is no reason why Stimpson couldn't have kept the "best" young men he had already screened and also screened and employed Ellen Church and the other "best" young women he interviewed. The conscious decision to create and reproduce a strictly racial-gender segmented labor force will have long-lasting implications for how the public views White womanhood as expressed via the ubiquitous imagery of flight attendants.

The first women flight attendants were judged by a myriad of factors, including their age and marital status. In 1930, executives at Boeing Air Transport (later United Airlines) put Ellen Church in charge of screening and hiring the first other nurse-stewardesses. The first stewardesses "had to be no more than 5"4 tall (to accommodate low airplane ceilings), between the ages of 20 and 26, weighing less than 118 pounds, and unmarried" (Vantoch 2013, 17). This pattern of assessing and barring women from employment on the basis of their age, weight, and marital status would endure in the airline industry for decades to come.

In the early years, the job was not glamorous, and flight attendants were expected to engage in considerable physical and interpersonal labor. Boeing Air Transport (later United Airlines) issued a training manual for stewardesses in 1931. In addition to cleaning cabins, heating coffee, creating reports on passengers and equipment, collecting tickets, caring for airsick passengers, and providing pillows, reading material, cigarettes, and gum, stewardesses were expected to learn each passenger's name, point out interesting geographical features along the way, and answer questions about the aircraft. Additionally, stewardesses loaded baggage, refueled planes, and rolled planes into hangars. In some instances, stewardesses even climbed onto the wing to help mechanics start the bulky engine (Vantoch 2013, 18). It merits noting that most of the skills necessary for this job were already well developed among the Black men who worked as Pullman porters. Based on this job description, there is every reason to assume that White women would be deemed unsuitable for this type of labor.

However, thousands of women applied for these positions, and competition was stiff for the job. For example, in 1939, the *New York Times* reported that American Airlines received five thousand applications for twenty job openings. The opportunity to travel without supervision, in addition to the decent wages and work conditions, clearly made the flight attendant job highly sought after. Given the restrictive gender norms of the time, this desire to fly away is certainly understandable. Stewardesses typically earned more than other White women working outside the home. In 1931, White women working in manufacturing earned roughly $60 a month, approximately half of the $100–125 flight attendants earned (Barry 2007, 29). Additionally, flight attendants also received paid vacations, free air travel, and an expense allowance during layovers. According to census data from 1939, average yearly income by race-gender were: White men: $1,419, White women: $863, Black men: $639, and Black women: $327. Clearly, employers did not turn to the cheapest laborers, Black women. This suggests that economic rationale alone was not a determinant of hiring decisions. In fact, the average monthly wage paid to Pullman porters between 1934 and 1935 was $73.25 (Berman 1935). This figure is considerably less than the $100–125 airlines paid flight stewardesses.

Job Requirements—Only Certain Types of Young White Women Need Apply

It turns out that only certain "types" of young White women would qualify to be flight attendants. As the job shifted from male-dominated (stewards) to female-dominated (stewardesses), the mere capacity to serve food was no longer enough. Officially, the stewardesses' job description can neatly be summarized as the following:

> A stewardess is an employee who is responsible for performing or assisting in the performance of all en route cabin service, or ground service to delayed or canceled passengers, which includes the responsibility for the welfare, comfort, enjoyment, and certain safety aspects of passengers. Stewardesses may from time to time be requested to participate in publicity and promotional assignments. (Stewardess Story)

However, as the job recruitment process would demonstrate, employers were in search of a specific type of woman. Based on an abundance of job advertisements, recruitment manuals, and secondary sources, we can discern the following constructions of the "appropriate" flight attendant: Specifically, age, weight, health, marital status, and sexual status were all key determinants of suitability for the job.

Although there were some slight variations across companies, flight attendants were typically between twenty-one and twenty-six years old when hired. Some airlines set the minimum age for women to be nineteen years old, while others set the maximum age to be twenty-eight years old. Male stewards, on the other hand, ranged in age from twenty-one to thirty-five (Stewardess Story). Even as late as 1954, American Airlines and others in the industry implemented an age maximum of thirty-two years old. At that age, flight attendants would be forcibly retired. (Vantoch 2013, 42).

In order to be employed as a stewardess in the airline industry, it was necessary that the prospective employees be in excellent health and pass a mandatory medical exam upon hire and at regular intervals thereafter. Possession of any physical handicaps or any visible scars or disfigurations disqualified an applicant. Similarly, flight attendants were required to have "teeth in good condition" and "good posture and appearance are prime requisites" (Stewardess Story). The preferred height for stewardesses was from 5 feet 2 inches to 5 feet 7 inches; the preferred weight was from 100 to 135 pounds (Barry 2007; Vantoch 2013).

Although airlines maintained a strict policy of barring married women from the attendant job, those that still hired men allowed them to be either married or single. Apparently, employers believed that the marital status of men, unlike women, should have a bearing on their employability. For example, "An applicant for the position of steward must be between 21 and 35 years of age. He may be either single or married" (Stewardess Story).

A Delta recruitment advertisement from 1940 asked for "Eight Hostesses: Can you qualify . . . Prefer Poise, Personality, Pulchritude." Alongside their nursing qualifications, Delta applicants were required to be "knowledgeable about current affairs and able to talk intelligently." Knowledge of the Atlanta Crackers, Delta's hometown team, an especially popular minor league team, was a particular advantage for recruits (Whitelegg 2007, 37). Similarly, an American Airlines press release of 1945 announced stewardesses' qualifications as "tact, courtesy and diplomacy, well-groomed, neat and attractive" (Vantoch 2013, 45). Employers demanded that flight attendants

> be a good, sincere listener. Ask leading questions and show interest in conversation. This allows the passenger the feeling of importance. Avoid talking about yourself and encourage passengers to talk about themselves. . . Avoid any type of conversation which is unladylike. (Omelia and Waldock 2003, 50)

The American Airlines stewardess manual of 1954 instructed stewardesses to care for the angry or hostile passenger by "loving him anyway." In short, the ideal stewardess was attractive, young, caring, congenial, and willing to tolerate abuse from unruly male passengers with a smile on her face.

Emotional Labor

Arlie Hochchild's classic study on flight attendants, *The Managed Heart: Commercialization of Feeling,* led her to coin the phrase "emotional labor." The practice of controlling emotions and outward manifestations in order to meet the emotional demands of a job is known as "emotional labor." Employers expect workers to explicitly control their emotions when interacting with clients, customers, coworkers, and managers. This includes regulating and suppressing emotions in response to the behavior of others. There was an expectation that flight attendants would smile constantly, whether those emotions were genuinely felt or not. Ultimately, employers' demand this emotional work from employees in order to evoke in the customer a certain emotion (satisfaction) that will enable the business to secure greater profits.

Sexual Purity

Flight attendants were also strictly warned about even the appearance of sexual impropriety with male employees. The first eight flight attendants hired by Boeing (later United Airlines) were cautioned that "One's personal conduct, especially in relation to members of the crew and other Boeing Systems employees, will be watched closely at all times, and any slight deviation with spoil the whole thing" (Vantoch 2013, 22). Also, "single" only meant never married. Divorced, widowed, and separated women were discouraged from applying for the job. Airlines were unabashed in proclaiming that they refused to hire married women. Airline executives believed and advertised that flight attendants were future wives-in-training. "Are you looking for a job that has. . . almost 100% chance for a husband in two years?" asked an American Airlines recruitment advertisement. As "matrimonial failures," with few exceptions, divorced women were deemed ill-suited for the job (Vantoch 2013, 44).

Upholding and Surveilling Beauty Standards

Once employers deemed the task of flight service to be "women's work," significant emphasis was placed on the appearance of stewardesses over time, As one United Airlines official told the *New York Times,* "You can run a $1.5 billion business, and it boils down to whether some chicks look good in their uniform." This statement highlights the extent to which managers believed that regulating the appearance of women's bodies was a prerequisite to profitability. "Attractive appearance will be paramount in the hiring of stewardess," outlined the supervisor's handbook for American Airlines in 1963. The statement was underlined because management considered it so important. The handbook further elaborated, "If a girl is beautiful, pretty, attractive, she has any woman's most effective attribute in dealing with the public. . . . That then, must be *our first consideration* in obtaining stewardesses." (Vantoch 2013, 112 italics mine).

The company's control over the flight attendants' appearance started during their training sessions. During stewardess training, women had weekly weigh-ins and "personal appearance" checks. A trainee could be dismissed simply for being one pound over the draconian weight restrictions (Vantoch 2013, 187). The extensive amount of beauty training underscores the extent to which airlines prioritized women's appearance. For example, in 1960, Pan Am devoted twenty-seven hours of stewardess training to grooming and only twenty hours to first aid. Similarly, American Airlines' six-week stewardess program totaled 120 hours, including 20 hours dedicated exclusively to beauty (Vantoch 2013, 115). In some companies, all potential stewardesses could expect to undergo a "beauty makeover." The makeover usually included a new hairstyle and makeup regimen. A former flight attendant recalled, "When we got back from our all-day beauty overhaul, we all burst into tears. We couldn't believe our eyes: we all looked alike—we were clones of each other!" (Barry 2007, 47).

In addition to making sure recruits did not surpass company weight limits,

> supervisors were trained to ferret out whether applicants had pretty legs and were forbidden from hiring women with 'large calves,' 'exceptionally thin calves,' or 'exceptionally large ankles.' During interviews, prospective stewardesses

> were asked to pull their skirts above their knees to display their legs and to walk across the room . . . (interviewers) measured her head, neck, shoulder, upper arm, wrist, bodice, waist, hips, upper thigh, calf, and ankle (Vantoch 2013, 113).

From a strictly utilitarian viewpoint of human capital, it is difficult to explain why the size of a woman's calf or ankles would have any bearing on her ability to perform the manual tasks associated with being a flight attendant. Clearly, women were being selected on the basis of how much they appealed to the "male gaze." In short, being considered attractive became a job requirement once women were installed in the role of flight attendant.

In addition to pre-flight patdown checks to ensure that all stewardesses were wearing their universally mandated girdles, employers' surveillance and management of women's bodies also included regular weigh-ins. Additionally, the emphasis on physical appearance was reiterated before every single flight. For example, before boarding, United Airline stewardesses were given the following checklist, asking them, "Is your . . . Smile friendly and sincere? Posture erect and poised? Makeup neat and natural? Nails manicured and polished? Ribbons new and trimmed? Gloves White and tailored? Hair short and styled?" (Whitelegg 2007, 42–43).

Recollections from flight attendants during this era underscore the controlling nature and absurdity of these requirements. "We all had to wear girdles," said Peggy Lee Baranowski, "I weighed 102 lbs and I had to wear a girdle!! They checked! They checked every aspect of our appearance and we had to comply" (Vantoch 2013, 110). Another flight attendant noted, "While on duty, we were required to wear a girdle. . .Our total appearance was observed at all times by our supervisors. Any hostess who did not meet standards could be sent home without pay" (Barry 2007, 47). Stewardesses were often put on probation, grounded, or fired for beauty infractions. Upholding the companies' weight restrictions became even more challenging for flight attendants after the 1950s, as thinness became more idealized for upper-class women (Vantoch 2013, 119). Airline executives' emphasis on the appearance of flight attendants continued for decades. Employers' emphasis on a standardized version of femininity was exemplified in a 1991 American Airlines flight attendant manual stating, "A firm, trim, silhouette, free of bulges, rolls, or paunches, is necessary for an alert, efficient image." (Barry 2007, 219).

From an essentialist viewpoint, the performance of White middle-class femininity is assumed to be an inherent manifestation of human biology. However, the case of flight attendants is reflective of the constructionist perspective. Namely, many seemingly "natural" gendered behaviors are learned throughout the course of our lives. Although passengers might experience flight service as a natural extension of women's nature, it clearly necessitated significant amounts of training and effort to perform this ideal of White femininity.

Training Women to "Act Like Women"

As airlines expanded their focus on passenger service, employers sought to manage and train this new workforce for the quintessential "White woman's job." American Airlines began the trend of instituting six-week stewardess training courses. In 1957, the company spent $1 million creating the first "stewardess college" on a twenty-two-acre campus that included classrooms, a kitchen, a dining room, and a beauty salon (Vantoch 2013, 105). A popular manual at the time, *How to Become an Airline Stewardess,* cautioned prospective flight attendants that "once your application for stewardess-in-training has been accepted by an airline, you become a student—not a stewardess—and attend a training school at the training center of the company."

This is usually located at their home base. These training classes last from approximately two to five weeks, depending on the company. "During training, you receive very little money from the company. They only attempt to allow "pin money," usually about $20 or $25 per week. It is suggested that the applicant bring enough money to live on for the length of the training period plus about three weeks thereafter (Stewardess Story). Additionally, stewardess training was notoriously grueling and strict. Women were booted daily for breaking rules and not meeting draconian airline standards. Every day, you'd see another empty desk. If you smiled wrong, you were out. It was bootcamp with White gloves and lipstick. We lived in fear." (Vantoch 2013, 186–187).

Personality coaching was a significant part of stewardess training. During flight attendant boot camp, stewardesses were taught patience and tact as a means to nurture and manage male passengers. Employers expected stewardesses to maintain an orderly cabin utilizing charm, thoughtfulness, and suggestion rather than force or threats. "Rather than blatantly displaying female authority, stewardesses were taught to exercise a refined performance of feminine tact to discipline unruly men" (Vantoch 2013, 41). (See figures 4.2, 4.3, and 4.4).

Breaking, Creating, and Reinforcing Race-Gender Norms (1930s–1960s)

By creating this new group of workers, employers were both reflective of, and challenging to, prevailing gender norms about White womanhood. The existence of a flight attendant was counter to the ideal that the daughters of respectable, White middle-class women should not work outside the home for wages. To be clear, such an ideal never applied to working-class women of any racial background. But the notion that men should earn enough money to prevent their daughters and wives from having to work outside the home was

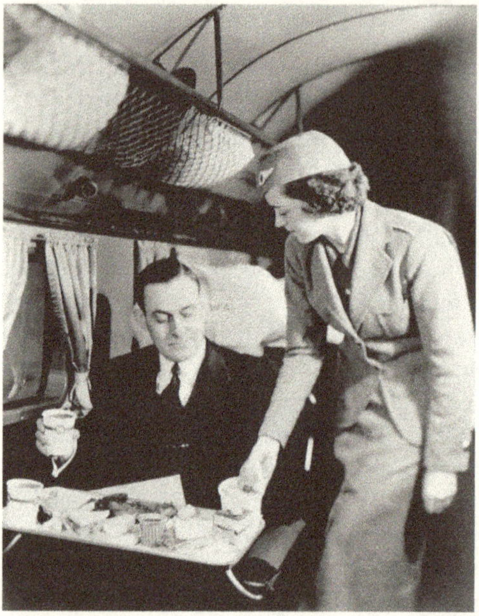

Figure 4.2 Flight Attendant Serving a Meal. *Source*: "Stewardess working." Catalog #: WOF_00108. Women of Flight Box 3. Diego Air and Space Museum Archive. Permission from San Diego Air and Space Museum.

Figure 4.3 TWA Stewardesses in Front of Plane. *Source*: "Stewardess in front of plane." Catalog: WOF_00109. Women of Flight Box 3. Women of Flight Special Collection. San Diego Air and Space Museum Archive. Permission from San Diego Air and Space Museum.

Figure 4.4 Pre-Flight Stewardess Responsibilities. *Source*: "Pre-flight Stewardess responsibilities." Catalog #: WOF_00098 Date: 1951. Item Location: Women of Flight Box 3. Collection: Women of Flight Special Collection. Permission of San Diego Air and Flight Museum.

part of the argument male-dominated unions made for a "family wage" (May 1982). Also, the idea of young women traveling and working independently, in the company of mostly men, was not reflective of existing notions regarding the (lack of) social and economic autonomy of White women.

Furthermore, these flight attendants were deemed courageous to enter the alien, uncharted territory of flying in a small enclosed vessel. These traits of courage and fearlessness did not map well onto the "damsel in distress" trope so ubiquitous in popular culture. Therefore, it can be argued that these women transgressed prevailing, traditional gender norms in a number of ways. On the other hand, the very presence of women in the job fundamentally transformed employers' definition and expectations of the flight steward. They now became "hostesses" in the air. By the late 1930s, serving others in flight had become a distinctly feminized job.

Although some airlines continued to employ male airline stewards, the majority of workers in the profession were women. The nurse-stewardesses first hired by airlines were reflective of a newer, respectable image of White working women. These women were depicted as the embodiment of "all-American" characteristics of hard work, discipline, and nurturing.

Employers explicitly made note of their preference for "girls from small towns" over their more "sophisticated" city-dwelling counterparts. Ostensibly because women from more rural areas were more likely to have "a good moral standing" (Vantoch 2013). This delineation thus reifies the dichotomy between "good" and "bad" women, sometimes referred to as the "virgin/whore" construction of femininity.

Employers' prohibition on employing married women is also reflective of hetero-patriarchal norms that married White men deserve to have a wife that is always available to tend to their domestic, emotional, and sexual "needs" at home. Company policies mandating the firing of a married flight attendant did not abate until decades later. After considerable acrimony, uneven collective bargaining efforts, and numerous cases filed with the Equal Employment Opportunity Commission (EEOC), in 1970, a federal court finally ruled that airline executives' ban on married flight attendants violated Title VII. Employers determined that being a flight attendant could only be a temporary job, not a source of long-term employment and career advancement. They did not relent on this stance until ordered to do so by a federal court ruling.

In 1936, there were 270 women and 1 man working as stewards on domestic airlines. Astoundingly, in the span of just five years, the occupation had gone from no-women to an almost exclusively female workforce. By 1940, 1,000 women were working as cabin attendants (Vantoch 2013, 25). In addition to hiring policies ensuring that women numerically outnumbered men by the mid-1930s, by then, the nature of the job itself had become more focused on the performance of White, middle-class femininity. Employers determined that traits such as charm, good cheer, attention to detail, a pleasant disposition, and concern with appearing physically attractive to a heterosexual male gaze would become part of the job itself.

Flight attendants rose to prominence in part because they embodied the new-wage earning woman and female domesticity. Stewardesses were educated, independent, industrious, attuned to the world, and focused on their careers. On the other hand, these White women were depicted as future housewives who served class-privileged White men in the sky as part of their training for a life of submissiveness (Vantoch 2013, 32). The following section discusses how the dynamics of White heteropatriarchy are reflected in the workplace dynamics aboard airplanes.

War, Piloting, and the Maintenance of Hegemonic White Masculinity

In the aftermath of World War II, airlines sought to make the connections between piloting, masculinity, and military dominance clear to the general public. Airline marketing was heavily influenced by mainstream American cultural roles. A first strategy was to tie airline logos to the Air Force and to emphasize their roles in the American military victory during World War II to create an image of masculine strength. As a means of tying flying with strength, airlines dressed flight crews in military-style uniforms. Pilots were projected with this virile masculinity by airlines, but rather than casting them as icons of out-of-control masculinity, they were positioned as strong, rational, and scientifically skilled men—a vision of masculinity that created an aura of safety for passengers who were afraid. After World War II, pilots also became "solid citizens and family men" who were married with children. By "casting the pilot as the epitome of middle-class masculinity post-war, airlines were appealing to the desire of male passengers to rejuvenate their manhood by reinventing manhood." Pilots embodied both suburban middle-class breadwinners and tough cowboys. In the 1950s, he was the quintessential family man (White, middle-class, corporate) who simultaneously reclaimed his manliness through frontier language and imagery (Vantoch 2013, 36–37).

Flight attendants were expected to perform deference to pilots. For example, in 1930, United Airlines' original "Do's and Don'ts" for "sky girls" demanded that "a rigid military salute will be rendered to the captain and copilot as they go aboard and deplane the passengers." (Omelia and Waldock 2003, 17).

Purchasing Your Own "Housewife in the Sky"

The tasks of a flight attendant were myriad, complex, and sometimes contradictory. She was the embodiment of domestic charm in the sky—caring, selfless, attentive, and personable. In order to succeed in their job, stewardesses were expected to maintain an unending supply of cheer and concern for passengers, from the first interview onward. The flight attendants worked very hard on what feminist social scientists call the labor of femininity, that is, they worked hard to have the body and express the emotions required of women according to White, middle-class, heterosexual standards (Barry 2007, 4).

> The nurturing required by airline service standards meant constant menial labor and emotional caregiving, qualities in tension with beauty, enchantment, and

> sex appeal . . . Coping with ill-behaved children, violent drunks, and panic-stricken travelers . . . The overarching ideal of femininity that flight attendants represented was an evolving blend of traditional domestic expectations and more modern ideals of attractiveness and charm on display—in other words, part glamor, part nurture. (Barry 2007, 6–7)

What employers and many customers expected from a stewardess was not dissimilar to what many White women experienced in the White-collar workplace. As so vividly depicted in the series *Mad Men*, employer's deemed the performance of gendered servility and sexual attractiveness as a job requirement for women to work as secretaries, clerks, waitresses, and even telephone switchboard operators. The difference is that flight attendants were widely marketed and depicted in popular culture. Therefore, it can be argued that the gender performances of stewardesses had more cultural resonance.

The ideal flight attendant was a mirror image of the ideal 1950s White housewife "who was good looking, a master at feigning interest in men's stories, eager to land and eligible husband, and ready to abandon her wage work to live out her true feminine calling as a full-time homemaker" (Vantoch 2013, 29). The airline industry depicted the airplane cabin as a reimagined suburban home where masculinity could thrive without domineering women. The introduction of male-only flights by United Airlines in 1953 is one example of this. It was common for men to indulge in a variety of "masculine" pleasures on "executive flights," including cigars, poker, and vulgar jokes. Playboy magazine presented these flights in 1955 as bachelor's clubs aloft, designed to bring back "the inner man." As Vantoch (2013) notes,

> United's logic for these flights: tired male executives needed to 'relax' in a 'manly fashion.' *Cosmopolitan* magazine applauded the flights for upholding traditional gender roles. Women appeared only to light their cigars and serve man-sized steak dinner[s]. The 'only girls aboard are a couple of unobtrusive stewardesses who encourage him to relax'. Stewardesses represented the best of female servitude by allowing men to behave as men (37–38).

Furthermore, ". . . her cabin is her 'sky home' where she reigns as a gracious, serving, considerate, imaginative, sparkling hostess who puts her guests at absolute ease and comfort" (41).

Branding and Marketing the Flight Attendant: 1940s–1960s

By the end of World War II in 1945, women's positionality in the airplane was well established. Women had served as pilots during the war under the Women Airforce Service Pilots program. But the program was abolished after the war, and women were once again shut out of the cockpit for another thirty years. Although the job of flight attendant had been numerically and performatively feminized, airlines did not initially make use of flight attendants as part of their marketing campaigns. Companies primarily focused on advertising the new technology, speed, and affordability of flying to businessmen. Analyses of airline advertising demonstrate that flight attendants did not emerge as a central part of the airline's branding until the mid-1940s. However, once executives determined that marketing the White femininity of flight attendants could prove profitable, the practice of including stewardesses in advertising became ubiquitous. During the 1950s, public relations professionals began to incorporate stewardesses more often in advertising and PR campaigns. Press conferences were organized with stewardesses to capture photographs on various occasions or whenever they had devised new statistics regarding the distance stewardesses walked on an aircraft, the quantity of bottles they had warmed for infant travelers, or the number of stewardesses who had retired due to marriage (Rosen 1987).

All of a sudden, flight attendants were seemingly everywhere in the media.

> As advertising became more sophisticated, airlines began to construct their own identity or "brand" around their flight attendants. The justification for having women on board shifted from alleviating fear to alleviating boredom, as new technology made long-distance flying increasingly viable but also increasingly uneventful. Airlines need to reinvent their workers as entertainers, a process that began during the ward and continued up to the 1970s. (Whitelegg 2007, 39)

The airline industry was eager to market flight attendants to the American public by deploying well-established advertising images about White female domesticity. As Vantoch (2013) notes, "the new stewardess icon derived from a popular archetype in advertising campaigns of the era—'the girl next door.' Postwar modeling agencies selected and groomed their models to fit this ideal by selecting "college girls, daughters of professors, young debutantes . . . who showed breeding, intelligence, and naturalness. The "typical American girl" was also, perhaps most importantly, a wife to be" (35).

Sexually Appealing but NOT Sexually Active

After World War II, airlines bragged about their pretty stewardesses, but despite the fact that these appealing women were geared toward attracting businessmen, they never painted stewardesses as blatantly sexual. Instead, they created a distinctly wholesome stewardess who was sexually attractive without being sexually delinquent. The image of the stewardess was derived from the popular "pin-up" girl of the 1940s. In 1941, Life magazine coined the term "pin-up" to refer to sexualized images of women displayed in men's lockers, bunks, and fighter planes. Millions of photographs of pretty women were sent to American soldiers in World War II, and the American public saluted these women as patriots who would boost their morale.

> She (pin-ups) garnered popularity not because she exuded an exotic sex appeal . . . but rather because she served as a model girlfriend, wife, and mother—exemplifying White, middle-class American womanhood. Her appeal sprouted from this wholesome image, which established her as a principal icon of moral obligation—the cherished "girl back home." (Vantoch 2013, 48–49)

> Airlines piggybacked on the popularity of the pin-up girl by incorporating aspects of her style into the image of the stewardess. In the early 1940s, TWA even hired famous pin-up illustrator George Petty to draw a TWA pin-up stewardess (large-breasted, blonde-haired, blue-eyes, and fully uniformed) that the airline used in counter displays, postcards, and baggage tags . . . The stewardess was a domesticated descendant of the pin-up who softened the sexual threat of the pin-up. (Vantoch 2013, 51)

"Coffee, Tea, or Me?"—Producing, Marketing, and Profiting from the Sexualization of Stewardesses (1960s and 1970s)

Airlines expressed concerns about the potential perception among their most valued clientele that air travel had become tedious and lacking in variety. The primary concern in the era of jet flights shifted from persuading the general public about the safety, exceptional efficiency, and growing affordability of air travel to addressing the issue of preventing boredom among experienced business travelers. Airline advertisers, in their pursuit of captivating and appealing to the disinterested frequent traveler, found inspiration not just from the innovative advancements in the advertising sector but also from the wider ongoing sexual revolution in the United States (Barry 2007, 99).

In 1960, the U.S. government approved oral contraceptives, which led to sweeping changes in sexual behavior and helped weaken the stigma associated with sexual activity outside of marriage and reproduction. Because the pill offered American women greater control over sexual activity and its repercussions, cultural producers utilized sex more often and openly for popular appeals (Barry 2007, 99–100). As Omelia and Waldock (2003) note, "in the 1960s', 'skirt lengths shortened, and sexist slogans grew'" (81). It was no longer risky for advertisers, including airlines, to promote the happiness and satisfaction customers would get from a product or service using sexual suggestiveness in the 1960s. Madison Avenue was increasingly blending personal and sexual messages. Airlines were especially equipped to eroticize their corporate personalities with young, single, attractive female bodies (Barry 2007, 100). During this era, mid-sized airlines, like Continental and

National, spent between $5 and $10 million a year on ads. Their larger counterparts, like United and American, spent upward of $20 million annually on advertising (Barry 2007, 99). The airline industry's most valuable customer in the early 1970s was still the businessman traveling on a business account, since more than three-quarters of passengers were in a professional or business occupation (Barry 2007, 100).

Previously, stewardesses were advertised as the all-American girl next door serving dinner to businessmen. However, by the mid-1960s, advertising depicted "stewardesses who performed in-flight stripteases. This bombshell stewardess in short shorts, fishnets, and go-go boots rapidly ascended to fame as a mythical American sex icon" (Vantoch 2013, 155). The advertisement prominently featured a stewardess in a provocative pose. For the first time, advertisements depicted stewardesses sporting long, disheveled hair. In the past, depictions of stewardesses did not often include establishing visual contact with the reader.

However, newer advertisements commonly portrayed stewardesses engaging in seductive gazes directed at the audience. Airline advertisements furthermore used a greater amount of sexual innuendo and provocative imagery pertaining to the physical attributes of the stewardesses. Stewardesses were seen in advertisements taking various casual and occasionally overtly suggestive attitudes, such as reclining down, dancing, placing their hands on their hips, and engaging in other similar actions. The tongues of stewardesses were even featured in advertisements. Displayed lying on the floor, these women appeared prepared for either social outings or sexual intercourse (Vantoch 2013, 180). Employers' transformation of the flight attendant from a future housewife, wholesome girl next door to a sex object was cemented by the late 1960s.

The attire of the newly appointed flight attendant was designed to elicit a sense of allure. Several prominent U.S. airlines implemented a policy change whereby they reduced the length of uniform hemlines to a range of one to three inches above the knee. Additionally, these airlines granted permission to their female flight attendants to adorn wigs, fake eyelashes, and other cosmetic goods that were previously prohibited due to their association with promiscuity (Vantoch 2013, 180). In 1967, Mary Wells, a prominent advertising executive, provided a concise and insightful description of her endeavors to enhance Braniff's brand perception inside the airline industry throughout the 1960s. Wells stated,

> When a tired businessman gets on an airplane, we think he ought to be allowed to look at a pretty girl. *A visual display of young, White, feminine allure had become an entitlement of the tired businessman*, who could attach to it whatever erotic fantasies he liked. (Barry 2007, 100)

Figure 4.5 1960s Flight Attendant. *Source*: "Debbie PSA Airlines_000137." Photo of Pacific Southwest Airlines History: San Diego Air and Space Museum Archive. Permission from San Diego Air and Space Museum.

In short, fantasies about young White femininity were part of a product for sale in the airline industry. Men were entitled to a sexual object as part of the ticket price. The apogee of this sexualization occurred in 1972 when National Airlines launched its "I'm Cheryl. Fly Me" campaign (figure 4.5).

What Place for Women of Color?

Producing and Commodifying Asian American and Hawaiian Femininity

In 1955, Pan Am expanded its Pacific routes and anticipated massive jet age expansion. They would staff these new routes with the first non-White flight attendants allowed into the industry. The airline announced its job criteria in both English and Japanese language publications in Honolulu, a city with a significant Japanese American population. The articles listed the following requirements: American citizenship; ability to speak, read, and write Japanese and English fluently; a height between 5 feet 3 inches and 5 feet 6 inches; ages twenty-one to twenty-seven; proportionate weight; single and not previously married; and either two years of college, nurse's training, or three years' work "contributing to poise and pleasant manner in dealing with the public" ("Pan Am to Employ Six Isle Nisei Stewardesses," cited in Yano

2011, 59). Pan Am hired Japanese American stewardesses purportedly for their language skills. However, in fact, many of the new recruits did not speak Japanese; plus, the airline served so few Japanese passengers at the time that Japanese language speakers were not actually necessary in flight.

Christine Yano (2011) utilizes the concept of "domesticated otherness" to explain how Nisei women, as members of a recently "enemy race," were incorporated into the ranks of flight attendants. The employer utilized prevailing ideologies about "Asian Femininity" to hire and market this on international flights after the Korean War. Resulting in part from the Korean War, during the 1950s, the image of subservient Asian "war brides" and "geisha girls" gained prominence in the media. Airline companies deployed this race-gender stereotype by hiring Asian American women as flight attendants on certain international routes. Airline executives utilized these Asian American women to highlight the exoticism and subservient customer service men could expect to receive on these international flights.

Drawing on stereotypes of Asian American women, "Pan Am publicized Japanese American stewardesses as subservient geishas, dedicated to pleasing men" (Vantoch 2013, 109). As Yano (2011) explains,

> the Euro-American image of the *geisha*—a highly sexualized figure whose existence centers around serving men—dominated the postwar view of Japanese (American) women. In fact, the geisha image can be seen as the exemplar of a host-guest relationship that points directly to the flight attendant profession. (Yano 2011, 22)

In the 1960s, United Airlines began employing muumuu-wearing Hawaiian stewardesses to facilitate an "exotic" and more authentic experience for its passengers. Company executives created a workplace policy that mandated these Hawaiian women sing, dance the hula, and play the ukulele in flight (Vantoch 2013, 109).

In summary, airline executives hired Hawaiian and Asian American women to perform a specific form of race-gender labor embedded within broader cultural ideologies about the exotic Orient. They sold the mostly male flying public on the image of a "domesticated geisha girl," intent on serving their every whim. The head of Pan Am from 1969 to 1972, Najeeb Halaby, referred to flight attendants as "geisha." He also suggested that the Japanese American (Nisei) stewardesses "should be more like Japanese geisha girls, prepared to flatter and entertain the male passengers" (Yano 2011, 22). To be clear, employers' hiring of Asian American and Hawaiian women was not an act of racial egalitarianism or colorblindness. Airline executives' obstinate commitment to upholding racial segregation and exclusion would be demonstrated in their treatment of Black women.

No Black Women Allowed

Working as a flight attendant was a highly sought-after position, employers systematically excluded Black women from the occupation until forced to do so in the mid-1960s. Although airline executives did not create explicit written policies forbidding the hiring of African American stewardesses, their practices consistently upheld racial segregation. It is critical to note that company executives did not willingly integrate the profession. In fact, employers spent a great deal of money and time upholding the racially segregated workplace they originally created.

Although employers were unwilling to openly admit to being racist and systematically barring Black women, airline executives provided various rationales for why they excluded Black women. One Northwest official asserted that they were "uncertain about the acceptance of a negro stewardess as a roommate by White stewardesses when the girls are required to share hotel rooms at turn-around points" (Vantoch 2013, 65). Other airline executives said they feared their White in-flight labor force would resign or demand higher wages if the job was integrated and the "psychological wage of Whiteness'' was eliminated onboard. In court proceedings, these airline executives worried that Black stewardesses would negatively impact ticket sales among their predominantly wealthy White passenger base. Donald Nyrop, the president of Northwest Airlines, confessed his position to investigators of the FEPC: "The time is not yet ripe to integrate Negroes into the stewardess positions." Northwest Airlines officials told the FEPC that they were "fearful that racially prejudiced passengers, particularly those from the South, might react unfavorably to the presence of a Negro in the position of stewardess" (Vantoch 2013, 64–65).

Although unwilling to admit to explicitly barring Black women from the flight attendant job, company executives readily provided myriad justifications for why racial segregation was necessary.

Two Exemplary Candidates—Not Good Enough!

Patricia Banks and Marlene White are two examples of Black women who exceeded all the written requirements for the position, except for one: their skin color. During the summer of 1956, Patricia Banks was a teenager at Queens College majoring in psychology . . . when she saw an advertisement for the Grace Downs Air Career School's stewardess program in *Glamour* magazine, she hopped on the train and applied. She scored in the ninetieth percentile on a test administered by the school and was accepted. A 95 percent average from the stewardess school made banks an exceptionally well-qualified candidate for the stewardess position. In addition to her extensive knowledge of airplane models, emergency procedures, meteorology, time zones, geography, charm, and other essentials for stewardesses, she also excelled in stewardess school, spoke French and Spanish, scored highly on intelligence tests, and played the violin. She was also light-skinned and extremely attractive by conventional standards. She was 5'6" tall, 120 pounds, and her figure measured 33-26-36, perfect measurements according to airline standards. Despite being a qualified candidate, Patricia Banks was denied entry into the flight attendant job (Vantoch 2013, 58–59). In 1957, Banks was rejected by Capital Airlines and submitted a discrimination claim to the New York State Commission Against Discrimination (SCAD).

The same year, twenty-four-year-old Marlene White applied for a stewardess position with Northwest Airlines. White was 5'4" tall, 112 pounds, and single, which was the minimum qualification for stewardesses on the airline. She was fluent in Spanish and French and had two years of college under her belt at the University of Detroit. White, who was the daughter of a Detroit magazine editor, was a young woman with aspirations. She had worked as a newspaper's society reporter and later received a master's degree in business administration from the University of Chicago. Not long after submitting her application for the stewardess post, she went on to become the cover girl for *Jet* magazine. When White contacted Northwest Airlines following her interview, a company representative informed her that the company did not hire African Americans for roles in flight (Vantoch 2013, 68). It is important to note that both Marlene White and Patricia Banks were light-skinned Black women with straight hair and closer to the Eurocentric beauty standards being applied. Both were eminently qualified to be flight attendants, yet they were still rejected solely based on race.

Airline executives continued to resist racial equality at every turn. In December 1958, New York State's SCAD finally succeeded in pressuring a regional carrier, Mohawk Airlines, into hiring Carol Ruth Taylor, a Black woman. It took over a year and a half for another Black stewardess to get hired by a U.S. airline company. "The select few African American women who would be hired shortly after . . . also had to win the position through discrimination lawsuits." (Vantoch 2013, 81). Although employers were eventually forced to curtail their racial discrimination, they fought the process every step of the way. In fact, "virtually no Black women were hired until after the 1964 Civil Rights Act was passed" (Douglas 2004, 161). In 1965, a grand total of fifty Black women worked as flight attendants, comprising 0.33 percent of the stewardess workforce. In 1970, only 2 percent of the nation's 35,000 flight attendants were Black.

There are several key findings that emerge from examining labor relations in the airline industry. First, airline executives created and maintained workplace segregation and hierarchies among workers. Second, employers did not select the cheapest available labor supply with experience in the transportation service sector, Black males. Third, it certainly was not self-evident that the job of serving passengers in the sky would eventually be reserved for White women. Fourth, once employers decided that being a flight steward was “White woman’s work,” their job expectations became highly gendered and sexist. Specifically, there was an increasing emphasis on physical attractiveness, strict surveillance of women’s bodies, employers terminating flight attendants’ employment upon marriage, and ultimately, the hypersexualization of the occupation. Fifth, employers obstinately utilized race and ethnicity as dividing lines. Asian American and Pacific Islander women were only allowed on certain international routes where they were meant to function as “exotic geishas.” Black women were barred from the profession. Employers did not willingly integrate the profession; their exclusion of Black women relented only after sustained pressure from civil rights organizations, governmentl agencies, and the courageous Black women who fought against this misogynoir.

While employers in the airline industry certainly were not colorblind, one could argue that the constrictions of the race-gender structure in the United States predetermined their hiring decisions. This begs the question: how do business owners respond when they have access to a global labor market? The modern cruise industry, which emerged in the 1970s, presents another case where we can examine employers’ decision-making regarding race, gender, and nationality among service workers. The modern cruise industry is a microcosm of global capitalism, wherein employers are free from the oversight of antidiscrimination laws or organized labor. Given this staggering amount of autonomy, it is especially fascinating to examine what type of workplace environment employers will create on cruise ships when left to their own devices. Will it be a post-racial, meritocratic system where workers are assessed solely on their capacity to perform a given task regardless of their nationality, race-ethnicity, or gender? What stories will employers tell regarding their different workers? Will they construct a narrative that legitimates colorblindness or one that upholds ideas of innate race-gender differences?

Chapter 5

Going Global

Service Work, Race-Gender-Nationality on Cruise Ships: 1970–2000s

On both trains and planes, the passenger's experience of service while being conveyed to a destination was central to what airlines were selling. The emphasis on service/servitude led to the personhood and social identity of the worker being foregrounded in passenger-worker interactions. Will the same process occur on cruise ships? The nature of work and labor hierarchies among a globalized workforce on cruise ships provides another case where we can examine the origins of race-gender segregation in the workplace and examine the justifications employers deploy to legitimize hierarchies among workers. In this chapter, we move from racial-gender structures bound by domestic U.S. structures and ideologies to a truly global system of categorization occurring on U.S.-owned cruise ships. This chapter examines the specific jobs and working conditions of service workers on these modern-day floating resorts. The role, if any, of race, gender, and nationality within the modern U.S.-owned cruise industry will be examined. Finally, to the extent possible, the stories management tells to explain workplace segmentation will be explored.

BACKGROUND—THE STATE, SERVICE WORKERS, AND LABOR LAWS

A "total institution" is a place "of residence and work where a large number of individuals, cut off from the wider society from an appropriate period of time, together lead an enclosed, formally administered round of life" (Goffman 1962). Ships, according to Goffman, epitomize institutions of complete control. For crewmembers, life aboard a cruise ship meets all the criteria Goffman specified for classification as a total institution. Almost all aspects of a crewmember's existence are controlled by the company—where/when they can eat, sleep, speak their native language, and leave the institution. There was and is no escape from corporate control for the seafarer aboard a cruise ship.

History of Oceanic Travel for Leisure

The paddle-wheel ship Quaker City's trip from New York in 1867 was most likely the first cruise that started in the United States. Charles C. Duncan, the cruise's organizer, described it as an "excursion to the Holy Land, Egypt, the Crimea, Greece, and Intermediate Points of Interest." The reason Mark Twain decided to join the voyage with 150 other "select companions" who would depart from New York and return six months later is why the advertisement drew his interest. For instance, after supper every night, visitors would stroll around the terrace, pray, and listen to organ music in the big saloon while reading and writing in their notebooks (Dickinson and Vladimir 2008, 4–5).

From the Quaker City era until the late 1950s, more individuals crossed the Atlantic out of necessity than choice. Immigrant travel between Europe and America, Great Britain, Australia, and New Zealand accounted for the majority of maritime transportation in the late nineteenth and early twentieth centuries. A growing number of individuals traveled across the Atlantic as trade and migration between Europe and North America expanded in the 1900s.

First-class cabins aboard opulent ocean liners were reserved for the affluent, who traveled in spectacular splendor while others did not. Their second- and third-class quarters were sparse, at most, lodgings with four or six beds and dormitory-style layouts, as well as overcrowded communal restrooms and baths (Dickinson and Vladimir 2008, 6).

The First Workers

International passenger travel on ocean liners for purposes of pleasure was largely a mono-racial affair. Service workers aboard vessels were mostly male. There are recordings of British seamen on passenger ships in the early twentieth century complaining about their difficult working circumstances (and for some, even the personal expenditure of buying the clothes and/or kitchen knives required to do their tasks). Cleaning common areas, serving meals, and setting up cabins were some of the most strenuous tasks assigned to stewards (Chin 2008, 114). Visitors who swarmed over the ship in their hundreds to admire its grace and beauty "never saw the glory hole," which the crew member shared with twenty-four other "tired-eyed and weary" boys who worked long days cleaning decks, polishing brass, and furniture "until everything was immaculate" and the ship was prepared to "hold court" with its admiring public. They worked seven days a week, had little shore leave, and never received overtime (Coons and Varias 2016). Unfortunately, little has changed regarding the conditions and low pay afforded to seafarers in the cruise industry.

Employers hired women to work as nurses, stewardesses, and telephonists on historic ships like the Queen Mary and Titanic, doing "women's work." However, they were incredibly few in number and, like their male counterparts, were almost exclusively White Europeans (Zhao 2002, 6). Women still comprise a minority of the workforce aboard a modern cruise ship and there are still certain jobs that are gender-typed. What has changed is the racial, ethnic, and national diversity of workers on cruise ships sailing out of the United States and Europe.

The Modern Cruise Ship Industry

The number of transatlantic passenger boardings gradually increased following World War II's conclusion, ultimately reaching its highest point in 1957. In 1958, Pan American introduced the inaugural nonstop transatlantic journey with a Boeing 707 jet aircraft. The crucial incident served as a decisive blow to the transatlantic cruise industry, leading to its decline in the 1960s. During the early 1970s, Carnival acquired the Mardi Gras, a vessel that boasted a size 50 percent greater than its competitors. This larger size allowed Carnival to provide a wide range of activities and entertainment options, catering to the diverse preferences of its passengers and ensuring an enjoyable experience for all. The adoption of the "Fun Ship" approach resulted in a paradigm shift where the ship itself assumed the role of the primary attraction while the ports of call were relegated to secondary importance, representing a complete departure from traditional cruise marketing strategies (Dickinson and Vladimir 2008, 28). With this move, an industry was reborn. U.S.-owned cruise ship companies have transformed themselves from small-scale, informal, debt-ridden entities into global behemoths. In 1977, the television show *Love Boat* was broadcast all over the world. The popularity of the show set onboard a cruise ship certainly helped generate awareness and interest in the previously downtrodden industry. Travel on cruises increased significantly between 1980 and 2001; the number of passengers on vacation cruise ships increased by 700 percent, from one and a half to twelve million passengers a year. By 2022, thirty-one and a half-million passengers embarked upon a cruise (CLIA 2023).

Data from 2022 show that three companies dominate the industry. Carnival Corporation remains the dominant company, with passenger and revenue market shares at 47.4 percent and 39.4 percent, respectively. They are followed by Royal Caribbean Cruise, with passenger and revenue shares at 23.0

percent and 20.2 percent, respectively. Last, Norwegian Cruise Line Holdings has passenger and revenue shares at 9.5 percent and 12.6 percent, respectively. These three companies control a global cruise market share of 80 percent in passengers and 72.2 percent in revenue (Syriopoulous et al. 2022). Globally, cruise companies owned approximately 200 ships and employed over 200,000 employees (CLIA 2023). It merits noting that these transnational corporations are working together across nation-state lines through the Cruise Lines International Association (CLIA). The CLIA works internationally to lobby governments that flagships, host ports, supply labor, and subsidize shipbuilding. These efforts have created a very business-friendly environment for ships to operate across the globe. For example, in 2013, Carnival Cruise Co., the industry leader, had $15 billion in revenue, $2.2 billion in profits, and a taxation rate of approximately 1 percent (Carnival Financial Report 2014). Just before the COVID-19 pandemic, the cruise line had hit record profits of $3 billion in 2019 (Wahba 2022). One reason for Carnival's immense profitability is their ability to utilize the "flags of convenience" system (discussed below) to circumvent domestic labor laws and regulations while operating on the high seas.

Passengers on Floating Resorts

Currently, cruising is mass-marketed as a floating resort that transports passengers to exotic destinations. Once limited to the upper and upper-middle classes, cruise vacations became affordable to middle- and even working-class Americans. For as little as $150 a night, one can purchase a room and unlimited food, enjoy live entertainment, and travel to a foreign destination. It is not uncommon for a contemporary cruise ship to contain multiple swimming pools, various restaurants, casinos, a movie theater, a skating rink, spas, dedicated areas and activities for children and teens, an arcade, a bowling alley, a rock climbing wall, and some even have a rollercoaster.

In 2019, North America remained by far the largest source region of cruise passengers, contributing more than half of global cruise passengers at 50.2 percent, Europe follows at 23.7 percent, and Asia trails at 15.0 percent. The Caribbean remains by far the prime cruise destination of high demand, at 32 percent, with the Mediterranean at 17 percent, and Europe (excluding the Mediterranean) at 11 percent (Syriopoulous et al. 2022).

Flags of Convenience System

Christine B. N. Chin's book *Cruising in the Global Economy: Profits, Pleasure, and Work at Sea* (2008b) is an invaluable resource on the history and political economy of the cruise ship economy. She notes that the majority of ships were governed by main or national ship registries throughout the first half of the twentieth century, which meant that crew members came from the ship owner's place of residence or citizenship and that the ships were built, registered, and flown under that nation's flag. All of these measurements were under one umbrella and were governed by extensive national laws. In what has been referred to for a few hundred years as the "global commons" of the oceans, ships bringing commodities and people operating. The attribution of nationalities to ships was and is still regarded as a means of enforcing order by entrusting responsibility to corresponding home governments, despite and precisely because of the open seas' fundamentally borderless environment (Chin, 2008b).

Historically, an ocean vessel owner had to register its "flag" with their home country. Meaning that the domestic country was responsible for creating maritime laws and overseeing the capital-labor relationship. In this way, capitalists and workers in the seafaring industry were bound to their "home" state. Because ownership and labor were mostly mono-national, the domestic nation-state mattered immensely. Citizenship provided workers with an institutional structure toward which they could direct their grievances and seek some protection. Starting in the 1960s, ship owners in Europe and the United States transferred their ships' flags from their nation of origin and operation to countries such as Liberia, Panama, and the Bahamas. Subsequently, Antigua and Barbuda, Bolivia, Cambodia, Equatorial Guinea, Myanmar, and Mongolia, among others, are also "flagging" countries (Chin 2008b, 38). In this globalized system, "ships may be built in one country, registered in another, their owners based in a third country, daily operations managed in a fourth country, and seafarers sourced globally" (Chin 2008a, 3). Coordinated efforts on the part of the cruise industry, in part through the CLIA, have successfully prevented any attempts in the U.S. Congress to alter the FOC regime (Garin 2006; Chin 2008a).

The "flagging" country then assumes responsibility for supervising and enforcing the ship's compliance with their national and international regulations on ship safety and working conditions. These countries charge registry fees and tonnage fees, but companies are not taxed on any of the revenue they generate on ticket sales, tours, and shipboard purchases. Under the current system, the cruise companies have considerable leverage over flagging states. As one shipping executive noted, "The chief advantage of the Panamanian registry is that . . . *we are under absolutely no restrictions*, so long as we pay the $1 net ton registry fee and 10 cents yearly a net ton tax" (Carlisle 1981, 10 italics mine). In addition to facing almost no restrictions, in some instances, companies are able to shape labor laws in ways that favor capital over labor. For example, in Panama, the cruise industry successfully secured a change in domestic law—workers' mandatory day off per week—is given at the company's discretion (Klein 2002). As cruise executive Bob Dickinson (2008) notes, "in truth, most flag-of-convenience countries have relatively few laws governing ship operations, which *allows the ships to operate under their own company policies and procedures*" (67 italics mine). In short, employers are unencumbered by antidiscrimination laws and organized labor. Without these hindrances, they are free to hire from a global labor pool and place those workers into the workplace hierarchy.

A Global Labor Force

In 2022, there were over 200,000 people from across the globe working on cruise ships. A typical cruise ship sailing out of the United States will contain workers from seventy to ninety different countries, the majority of whom are from the Global South. Those laborers performing both the invisible work below decks and the customer-facing service interactions are recruited almost exclusively from "poor countries" in Asia, Eastern Europe, Latin America, and the Caribbean. This global supply of labor is procured through the use of independent crewing agencies all over the world.

Officers, Staff, and Crew

Onboard cruise ships, nationality is the primary determinant of an employee's placement within the immensely hierarchical structure of cruise ships. Although there are exceptions, there is a striking correlation between workers' pay/status and their countries' position within the global economy. A report produced by the International Transport Workers Federation (ITF) succinctly describes the hierarchical structure of cruise ships:

> The by-and-large White passengers from the industrialized countries, the Master and his senior officers, and staff enjoy the luxury of the upper decks, with service staff to fetch and carry on a 24-hour basis. The higher status employees, largely from industrialized countries, have cabins—often above the water-line. They eat at their own waitress-served restaurants, have their sheets changed every day, and often have access to passenger facilities (internet café, pool, spa, etc). Meanwhile, below decks, the majority are from developing countries and Eastern Europe. They sleep in cramped, noisy cabins. Their food is often leftovers, taken in a crew canteen. In effect many rarely come above the water line when at sea. Those from industrialized countries, by contrast, rarely work below decks unless they are skilled maritime crew or supervisors. (ITF 2002, 12)

While there are some deviations, officers and staff members are usually from the Global North and crewmembers are from the Global South. The division of labor aboard, job expectations, the nature of work, and crewmembers' experiences will be the focus of the following section.

A ship is akin to a paramilitary organization. Officers dress in uniform. The way things are done is heavily influenced by laws, rules, rank, and discipline. Each person has a certain rank and set of obligations. The workers may be disciplined if tasks are not carried out as directed. In this line of work, following rules and instructions is how you advance (Dickinson and Vladimir 2008, 69). The hierarchical shipboard social system has the captain, sometimes known as the "Master," at its peak. The captain has the last say in all matters on board. It is notable that the authors stress that captains must be attentive to the diversity of their staff.

> A good captain is aware of the crew's varied cultural heritage. Therefore, he fosters a climate of courtesy and respect for every member of the crew, regardless of their position, color, nationality, political views, religious beliefs, or sexual orientation. The training manual stresses that bigotry, hostility, partiality, and intolerance are all unacceptable behaviors to him. (Dickinson and Vladimir 2008, 71)

Even senior officers, such as a captain have distinct managerial expectations that involve a measure of emotional labor. They are required to be "nice" and "smile" to the passengers since the captain and other senior officers are allowed to participate in social events in the passenger area. For instance, the captain is required to host social meals at the captain's table twice a week as the ship's master. During the dinner, the captain "socializes" with a dozen carefully chosen passengers by conversing with and grinning at them. He must snap photographs with hundreds of dressed-up passengers on every weekly trip. The man must control his feelings and emotions in order to maintain his smile, meeting passengers, shaking hands with them, and posing for them during the performance (Zhao 2022). Captains certainly engage in "emotional labor" and must regulate their feelings and maintain a cheerful demeanor in public. What distinguishes their emotional work from that of porters and flight attendants is that captains are never expected to be subservient to passengers. Furthermore, captains are in a position to demand deference from their subordinates, the entire workforce, on a whim. Lastly, captains are able to retreat and return to the workplace. Typically, captains and other managers spend four months on board a ship, followed by two months of paid vacation at home (Dickinson and Vladimir 2008, 79).

The hotel manager employs the largest personnel aboard the ship. The administration of food and beverages, hotel operations, entertainment, gift shops, spas, and casino operations fall under the purview of the hotel manager's functional responsibilities. The hotel manager receives reports from the food and beverage manager, who oversees the hotel's eateries and bars, as well as the executive chef and housekeeping manager (chief steward). Lastly, there is the ubiquitous cruise director, who is in charge of all the ship's entertainment staff. During the evening, cruise directors may be seen all around the ship, monitoring everything from the main acts that are being performed in the show lounge (which they often introduce), the pianist performing in the piano bar, the DJ performing in the nightclub, the comedian performing in another lounge, and the teen party that is taking place in the teen club (Dickinson and Vladimir 2008, 89). Cruise directors come from a variety of backgrounds but are mostly from North America and Western Europe.

Staff

This group includes singers, dancers, musicians, exercise and yoga instructors, shore excursion managers, youth activity directors, a newsletter editor, and, on certain ships, a print shop and television studio. Additionally, the purser's personnel run the reception desk, which is located at the ship's middle. This is where travelers go to get information, file grievances, and handle financial issues. Customs and immigration are two other significant responsibilities handled by the purser's office. When describing this segment of the workforce, the former CEO of Carnival, Bob Dickinson, and his coauthor assert, "On the major lines, *the purser's staff is often American because these jobs appeal to U.S. citizens and aren't regarded as servile*" (Dickinson and Vladimir 2008, 81). This quote begs the question: If U.S. citizens are not suitable for "servile" (read: crew) jobs, who is?

Customer-Facing Crew Members

Unlike cruise staff and purser's personnel, who mostly hail from the United States and Western Europe, crew members almost exclusively come from the Global South. In their descriptions of crew members' work, it is clear that Dickinson and Vladimir acknowledge that shipboard labor is incredibly onerous for workers on cruise ships. Passengers are the only party deliberately shielded from understanding this harsh reality behind the sparkling facilities and abundant food supply. In the next section, crew members' experiences and the nature of various jobs are discussed.

Many passengers consider food to be one of the most important components of the cruise. Delivering food to 3,000 passengers is a monumental task that occurs in formal dining rooms, restaurants, buffets, bars, and cafes. This all necessitates constant staffing by food and beverage workers. It is worth noting that waiting tables on a cruise ship require more effort than a routine one-time encounter between customer and waitstaff. Employers expect that wait staff will commit passengers' preferences to memory and attempt to forge a personal relationship with the customer. Dickinson and Vladimir acknowledge that serving food on a cruise differs from other contexts because the group of customers remains the same for a whole week or longer.

> This enables the worker to develop a relationship with the guests so that he can improve his service to them. For example, after the first night, when the waiter asks you whether you prefer coffee or tea, he should not have to ask you again . . . remembering the details, developing a relationship with passengers, and having a real service attitude become the most important thing. It is hard work—our waiters may work as many as twelve hours in a sixteen- or eighteen-hour period. Because it's in shifts, they get an hour or two off in between. (Dickinson and Vladimir 2008, 84–85)

This type of personalized service is demanded by the company while paying workers very little.

Cabin stewards are expected to clean rooms impeccably, and "they need to tell them (passengers) to have a nice day, ask them if they need anything, and get it if they do. I expect them to offer to press their clothes for the captain's party and to make sure the passengers know them by name" (Dickinson and Vladimir 2008, 87). These work requirements are reminiscent of the physical and psychological demands placed upon porters. Cleaning rooms is just one of the tasks required of these workers. Similar to the Pullman porter, management expects stewards to perform domestic labor while simultaneously forging a relationship with customers and being attentive to their desires.

Performing Good Cheer and Servility

Workers are expected to do much more than perform the routine tasks of serving food and cleaning rooms. Instead, managers expect crew members to also entertain and give customers personal service, all for extended periods of time, for low pay. Employers train workers to offer supplementary embellishments or unforeseen elements. For instance, a room steward is responsible for skillfully arranging towels into various animal shapes on a nightly basis. The waiter has the potential to engage children of all age groups by offering magic tricks or performing illusions with their napkins. Oftentimes, waitstaff will also demonstrate the techniques to interested passengers at the table. During most evenings during the duration of the trip, it is customary for the waitstaff to engage in singing and parading activities within the dining area. For example, on Carnival trips in the Caribbean, "Hot! Hot! Hot!" by Arrow is often played in the dining room. This lively tune has the remarkable ability to engage a significant number of attendees, prompting them to participate in the dance procession as both guests and staff navigate through the eating area. "Waiters with trays of drinks balanced on their heads lead the parade while performing amazing limbo contortions" (Dickinson and Vladimir 2008, 113).

In this light, the expectations placed on food service workers on cruise ships mirror and exceed the obligations of a flight attendant or Pullman porter.

Employers' insistence that porters and flight attendants always appear to be happy and constantly smiling extends to crew members as well. A smiling service worker is a vital component of the product or service that cruise lines promise to deliver to meet their customers.

Similar to the ways porters and flight attendants were utilized by employers, travel brochures and advertising often features the smiling faces of crew members of all colors.

> These smiling faces are presented to convey a message or to leave an impression: on cruise ships seafarers enjoy their work as much as passengers enjoy their fun and leisure. "It's a heaven not in this world!" as put by one of the major cruise lines in its television advertisement. (Zhao 2002, 7)

The smiling faces of these workers, mostly from the Global South, concealed the reality of hard labor behind the scenes and their lives in cramped quarters below decks. Employers' emphasis on workers constantly appearing to be happy servants remains a hallmark of the job.

Starting in the late 1990s, the cruise line began demanding more "quality service" from crew members. In an interview, a human resources manager of a major cruise shipping company noted,

> [W]e not only want our crew to keep the cabins clean, but to serve the passengers with right wines and right foods. These material aspects are certainly important. But we also want our crew to maintain the right attitude. They must always remember, this is part of the hospitality industry and *they must help the company keep our guests happy, and they can do this only by keeping themselves happy, and demonstrate it to our guests through their service and attitudes.* (Zhao 2002, 10)

Given the arduous conditions employers have imposed upon crewmembers, it is especially galling that these workers are expected to compel themselves to feel and display happiness all the time. The notion that workers, in all instances, must constantly be smiling and pretending to be cheerful, so their employer can earn more money, is a standard few people would willingly impose upon themselves.

The majority of customer-facing service occupations require a certain degree of emotional labor. Nevertheless, service occupations exhibit considerable diversity in several aspects, such as remuneration, working conditions, duration and expectations of subservience, amount of monitoring, reliance on a living wage vs. gratuities, and the capacity of workers to challenge their degradation without jeopardizing their employment.

Table 5.1 Salaries/Vacation for Select Ship Positions

Position	Monthly Salary (in $)	Work Duration (in Months)	Vacation Time (in Weeks)	Paid Vacation (Yes or No)
Captain	5,000–6,000	3–4	2–5	Yes
Chief Officer	3,750–4,200	3–4	2–5	Yes
Hotel Manager	3,800–4,700	3–4	2–5	Yes
Staff (entry level)	1,000–1,300	6	4	Yes
Executive Chef	4,300–4,870	3–5	4–8	No
Waitperson*	50 (plus tips)	6–9	4–8	No
Busperson*	50 (plus tips)	9–12	8–12	No
Cabin Steward*	50 (plus tips)	9–12	8–12	No
Laundry Person	400-600	9–12	8–10	No

Source: Chin 2008b.
*Average reported monthly earnings (wages and tips) for waitpersons are $1,500–2,220, buspersons earn $1,000–1,500, and earnings for cabin stewards are not reported.

Wages and Reliance on Gratuities

Reminiscent of the stark inequities witnessed in the Pullman case, remuneration on cruise ships is incredibly inequitable as demonstrated in table 5.1.

Echoing the arguments deployed to justify forcing porters to rely on tips, employers in the cruise industry admit that tipping is utilized as a disciplinary measure to ensure that food and cabin service workers remain sufficiently servile. According to former Carnival Company CEO, Bob Dickinson,

> The danger of a no-tipping policy, especially in service industries like hotels, restaurants, are cruise ships, where you tend to have a large number of low-salaried employees, is the inherent risk of poor service when the staff isn't motivated to perform at their highest level to earn tips and thus increase their income! (Dickinson and Vladimir 2008, 230)

This discourse deployed to justify why crew members must rely on tips for a sizable portion of their income is eerily similar to Pullman executives' reasoning regarding porters.

The Stories Employers Tell: Legitimizing Inequality Among Crewmembers

Strikingly, employers in this context do not explain their recruitment and hiring processes in colorblind, race-neutral language. On the contrary, the ethnic and gender identity of the worker is assumed to be reflective of their suitability to work as a crewmember. Employers appear to imbue men and women from different ethnicities/races/nationalities with certain inherent characteristics that manifest themselves in the personhood of different workers. There is no pretense to merely assessing atomized individuals with varying degrees of human capital; in this instance, employers assert that the cultural background of the worker determines their capacity for service.

Since company records are not archived, as is the case with railroads and airlines, data on employers' national-race-gender ideology is gleaned from scholarship that has conducted interviews with managers and a book cowritten by Bob Dickinson, formerly the CEO of Carnival Cruise Company.

An interesting finding was the way U.S. citizens of all racial backgrounds were deemed inherently unsuitable to work as crew members. Rather than explain the absence of U.S. citizens as a result of low wages, incredibly long hours, and extended periods of time away from home, cultural explanations are provided by employers. "The egalitarian nature and heritage of Americans tend to work against their ability to be motivated to serve others" (Dickinson and Vladimir 2008, 67). They go on to say, "On major lines, the Purser's staff are often Americans because these jobs appeal to them and aren't regarded as servile" (Dickinson and Vladimir 2008, 81). The viewpoint just described is particularly problematic because it implies that there is a group of people, namely, workers from the Global South that are naturally suited to serve others under these harsh conditions.

Gender Dynamics

The workforce composition on modern cruise ships reveals that women make up around 20 percent of the total employees. Their presence is predominantly seen in the hotel division of these ships, where they are primarily engaged in two types of roles. First, they undertake the "frontline" responsibilities that include direct interaction with guests. Second, they are involved in the "backstage" tasks related to cabin cleaning. The shipboard placement of women is partially influenced by the criterion of physical appearance, particularly for certain non-officer roles such as receptionist, cabin and restaurant steward, masseur, and hairdresser (Chin 2008a, 13). Similar to the flight attendants, women crewmembers are ranked based in part on their attractiveness.

Although women of different racial, ethnic, and national backgrounds can be found working on the ship, there remain stark divides among them. Women from North America and Western Europe work as "staff" members and are more likely to consider working on cruise ships as a chance to make tax-free money for a few years while also approaching the job as a form of tourism. On the other hand, women from Southeast Asia and Eastern Europe are usually "crew" members who are working aboard the ship out of financial necessity (Chin 2008a, 13). Even though their motivations differ, female employees are often considered more naturally amenable to service work. As a captain with twenty years of experience working on cruise ships, opined that,

> In service, I think, girls have better criteria than men, the men are more steady, last more hours, but the women are unique in this thing, they are better, it's their nature. So if you put this in a whole I find they are equally performing. For example, *in housekeeping you can take the type of the typical British butler like you've seen in the movies, how many of them can you find to make a cabin look luxurious and always with a smile?*
>
> *You can't find many, because it's not in a man's nature.* But you can find many girls who can make a cabin look beautiful, nice and cozy, and they smile better, it's their nature. (Zhao 2002, 15 italics mine)

It is noteworthy to observe that these gender beliefs possess a tendency to reinforce themselves. Employers see women as possessing more social skills, leading to their frequent employment in roles that involve regular customer interaction within the maritime industry. Consequently, the overrepresentation of women in these frontline jobs is then perceived as indicative of inherent disparities between males and females. A similar process occurs with Filipino men.

The Case of Filipino Men

As was the case with the porter, "the ascription of the service trait to Southeast Asian men has an effect of 'feminizing' them in comparison to the more 'masculinized' identity of, and work performed by, cruise ship officers and managers from Western and Eastern Europe" (Chin 2008a, 13). William Terry's (2014) is especially relevant to the discussion of racialization in the cruise industry, particularly in regards to Filipino men. Although cruise lines are able to recruit from around the globe, certain nationalities are more predominant than others. Globally, Filipinos accounted for roughly 30 percent of all cruise ship workers in the early 2000s. There are a myriad of economic, political, and social factors that have compelled large numbers of Filipino workers to seek work outside the country. However, when explaining the overrepresentation of Filipino men in hotel and food service work on cruise ships, employers often reference the supposedly innate qualities they possess.

Similar to porters and flight attendants, once a decision is made to hire workers from a particular group, employers develop a narrative as to why they are naturally suited for a certain role. As Zhao (2002) found in their research, employers continue to tell stories that explain why some people are born to be servants. An interviewee noted,

> Somehow, the Asian seafarers, especially the Filipino . . . *seem to have been born with a wonderful service culture. They always greet the guests and always smile. And, they do it so naturally.* They always look energetic, positive and cheerful, even after 9 months at sea! In comparison, European seafarers seem easy to get fatigued. After 4 months, their fatigue will show, and our guests don't like to see those who serve them look tired and cannot smile. (Zhao 2002, 11)

The assertion that Asian people are naturally more cheerful and capable of arduous labor compared to Europeans is certainly a stereotype that serves to explain why they are overrepresented in certain jobs.

> To argue that some are *culturally* better suited to serve others under conditions of fluctuating monthly income, long work hours, and no rest days or paid vacations is to relegate them to a permanent status of relative servility that, somehow, absolves management from the responsibility of, or need to, improve terms and conditions of work at sea. (Chin 2008a, 15)

The stereotype that Filipinos are innate seafarers is another example of a discourse that seeks to legitimize ethnically stratified employment decisions. In actuality, the Philippines has not always contributed a sizable number of employees to global maritime trade, and it did not instantly overtake other seafaring nations as the top provider of labor. Only a small percentage of Filipinos may have been seen working on foreign ships as recently as the middle of the twentieth century (perhaps on U.S. Navy ships). They only started to significantly contribute to the international maritime labor force in the 1970s, when the Marcos dictatorship built the state migration machinery. "Yet, the suggestion that Filipinos are naturally suited to seafaring because they reside in an island nation is often among the first explanations one is given when speaking with industry insiders" (Terry 2014, 74). The idea that Filipinos are innately and biologically designed to work as seafarers seems to provide an advantage to Filipinos when seeking a job as a hotel or restaurant crew employee.

It warrants noting that this reductionist discourse can also be espoused by Filipino crewing agencies. According to a manager whose agency supplies labor to a major cruise line, the reason employers seek out these workers is,

> the first thing is the English language . . . . . . Next is the attitude of the Filipinos, and positive attitudes in terms of their dedication to work. *Filipinos are*

> *obedient, resilient, happy people Even our ancestors are more of the seafarer type of people, it runs in the blood.* (Terry 2014, 83 italics mine)

While aiding in gaining access to employment on board, these stereotypical beliefs about them, placed them toward the bottom of a hierarchically ordered workforce.

Feminizing their work and ideologies about their innate cheerfulness and docility made it harder for Filipino men to advance in the occupational hierarchy. A European labor recruiter interviewed by Terry (2014) asserted,

> With balance, Filipinos are hardworking and reliable and will go to the limit with you; *they are subservient.* Europeans generally occupy leadership roles on cruise ships because they show more attention to details, whereas Filipinos must be disciplined in order to function well. (Terry 2014, 85 italics mine)

The idea that Filipino men are naturally suited for servitude and need supervision is reminiscent of ideologies used to justify Black men's confinement to the porter role. However, unlike porters, who were barred from becoming conductors, some Filipino men can climb the occupational ladder even though they face a glass ceiling.

"Whiteness" in Its Various Forms—The Case of Eastern Europeans

Since the latter part of the twentieth century, individuals from Eastern Europe have been enlisted to serve as employees on cruise ships controlled by management in the United States. The integration and employment of Eastern Europeans aboard cruise ships were characterized by their placement and associated identity within the complex framework of nationality, race/ethnicity, and social class. According to one maritime lawyer, "the Eastern Europeans are the new slaves of choice . . . the cruise industry likes them because they are light-skinned, have Romanesque features and will work for peanuts [80-hour work week at $1.56 an hour]." (Chin 2008a, 11). In addition to being a cheap source of labor, employers' placement of Eastern Europeans was not random. For example, in 2003, Holland America announced a new initiative for its "Pinnacle Grill," a specialty restaurant where guests paid an extra fee to enjoy signature gourmet food. The Indonesian and Filipino waiters who staff the main restaurants, who had more work experience, were excluded from working in the upscale restaurant. The Pinnacle Grill was staffed by a dozen Hungarian waiters, and the company planned to transition to European service personnel in this specialty venue on other ships. Apparently, White skin conveyed a higher status than Brown to employers seeking to profit from an additional revenue stream. The senior vice president of fleet operations, Stein Kruse, stated, "There's no question our traditional staff are extremely competent. Employing European servers is simply a way of further differentiating the Pinnacle Grill from the main dining room'" (Garin 2005, 198). It is important to note that being Eastern European did not preclude a worker from being placed in a low-status position on the ship.

However, White European faces are still an important component of the image cruise lines seek to maintain. Given the high labor costs of hiring White women from the United States or Western Europe, cruise lines turned to cheap labor from Eastern Europe to maintain their professional image of Whiteness. Employers utilize women from this region to work "front of house" jobs, such as reception and greeting passengers in public areas. "These places are considered to best represent the visual image of the cruise line as well as the best selling points." Zhao's interview with a retired caption still actively serving on the management board of a major cruise shipping company: "But there are jobs for which you will need Europeans . . . they represent the classical image of the industry" (Zhao 2002, 16). In short, Whiteness is an essential part of the corporate image, even though workers from the Global South are in the majority.

"Dividing and Conquering" or Embracing Multiculturalism?

It can be argued that a "divide and conquer" strategy has informed the U.S.-owned cruise ship industry's organizational structure and recruitment strategy post-1981. The strike of Easter Sunday, 1981, was a watershed moment in the cruise industry. Prior to this incident, workers were recruited primarily by word of mouth from existing workers. A social network of siblings, cousins, and friends of existing workers were brought aboard to fill job vacancies, thereby creating cohesive groups of crewmembers. This strategy of recruitment would be abandoned permanently after the strike. Approximately 240 Honduran workers went on strike aboard a Carnival Cruise ship in the port of Miami to protest the firing of two coworkers. The strike was spontaneous and unorganized, but militant. The workers managed to shut down operations on the boat for several days. Carnival's owner hired a small army of ex-paratroopers from Wackenhut (the company that currently runs private prisons), and along with the Immigration and Naturalization Service—they stormed the ship, declared the strikers illegal immigrants, and promptly shipped them back home. Worried that a cohesive network of workers could once again disrupt operations, the industry changed recruitment tactics and goals. Crewing agencies—dispersed across the globe—became the sole recruiting mechanism. This way, workers from various nations, with no previous ties to one another, would be randomly mixed across crew jobs. As one senior executive from Carnival acknowledges, "the whole thing (goal) was not to have a ship with 15 percent or more of one nationality" (Garin 2005, 196).

The cruise industry is ingenious because it conceals its divide and conquer strategy under the guise of "multiculturalism." The cruise ship company itself celebrates pluralism and uses it as a marketing device, as an aspect that enhances the cruise experience. Wearing name tags with the employee's nation of origin is required for all crew members. These badges are a visual inscription of each worker's national identity and a means of making diversity more pronounced. To be sure, it is a rarity to share a physical space with people from ninety different countries, and this unique experience itself is often marketed in an onboard newsletter. In addition to the prominent name tags, it is a common practice for the cruise director to announce during orientation the number of nations represented by the staff and to refer to them as "mini-United Nations."

However, because the cruise industry could fill its staffing vacancies by relying on workers from fewer countries (as they did prior to 1981), there is reason to be highly skeptical that employing workers from seventy-five to ninety different countries has anything to do with celebrating "diversity." Aside from wearing a name tag with their country of origin listed, workers are prohibited from doing anything that actually reflects their cultural background. For example, workers are expressly prohibited from conversing in their "native tongue" around passengers. This is not to say that current company executives, management, and recruiters are sitting in offices, cognizant, and actively plotting to keep workers divided in a deeply hierarchical workplace. As previously discussed, organizational inertia can reproduce these dynamics in the absence of overt intentions on the part of company executives.

In summation, cruise companies founded in the United States during the 1970s have grown into massive transnational corporations that enjoy minimal government oversight, a large pool of cheap and disposable labor dispersed across the globe, high profit margins, and minimal taxation. While these companies are largely free from state regulation, they manage to exert significant influence over the policies of governments in the Global North and South. The lack of labor organizing has also created a situation wherein companies have almost complete control over a vast labor force recruited primarily from Asia, South and Central America, the Caribbean, and parts of Eastern Europe. The nationalities represented by capital and labor originate from tens of different countries and are unique in their confinement to a singular, contained workplace. However, in both practice and discourse, cruise ships replicate patterns of racialized servility and hierarchies of color, which date back to colonialism. Specifically, mostly White men from the Global North are at the top of the *onboard workplace* hierarchy and are racialized as possessing the qualities necessary for leadership and dominance over others. Workers from the Global South, especially Southeast Asian men, are racialized as naturally suited for servility on board the ship.

The "Hegemony of White Masculinity" and the New Faces of Leadership

Unlike the previous two cases, Whiteness and maleness no longer ensure that a worker will not be subjected to the authority of a woman or racial "Other." In fact, in 2013, Arnold Donald, a Black man and New Orleans native, succeeded Micky Arison, the billionaire son of the company's founder, as the CEO. A seasoned executive at Monsanto, Donald had served as a Carnival board member for twelve years prior to his appointment. After successfully steering the company through the COVID pandemic, he left the role in 2022 and was subsequently replaced by a White man, Josh Weinstein. From 2015 to the present (2024), a White woman, Christine Duffy, has served as the president of Carnival Cruise Lines. This is certainly a positive development for those individuals and those seeking more diversity in the upper echelons of corporate America. However, their presence has not undone existing patterns of inequality. The final chapter of this book discusses the changes and continuities in race-gender inequality in the workforce.

Chapter 6

Conclusion

Some Things Change, Others Stay the Same

It is indisputable that individuals of any color, ethnicity, country, and gender have the capability to undertake the responsibilities related to transportation service employment. Individuals of various racial-ethnic backgrounds and genders may evidently carry out the act of providing service to others. However, it seems that the identification of those who engage in such labor influences the expectations for the qualities and performance associated with the employment. For example, "Geisha girls" adorned in traditional attire; Hawaiian workers engaging in hula dance; African American males, displaying their vocal talents, expressing contentment in their subservient roles; White women, assuming the roles of "housewife in the sky" and subsequently being objectified as sexual beings; and Filipinos, perpetually wearing smiles and demonstrating their "innate" willingness to provide service. The concepts surrounding White heteropatriarchy are continually manifested in many aspects, such as compensation, job security, qualifications, and so forth.

Racism and sexism are sometimes mischaracterized as issues predominantly emanating from the working class. The notion that less-educated White males are the main propagators of prejudice continues to hold considerable influence throughout both the left and right political spectrums in the United States. It is worth acknowledging that exclusive country clubs were among the final establishments to undergo integration (Jolly-Ryan 1998). The instances of both the railroad and airline industries illustrate that individuals belonging to the elite White male demographic had a significant role in establishing the workplace hierarchy based on race and gender, as well as being the key customer base whose preferences required careful consideration. When implementing discriminatory employment practices based on race and gender, these companies were not yielding to the influence of organized White employees or seeking to appease the regressive ideologies of the general population. Moreover, throughout the period spanning from the 1880s to the 1960s, the clientele utilizing train and air travel predominantly consisted of those occupying executive positions within the respective companies. Once again, those belonging to the privileged demographic of White males hold positions of power and influence. If one posits that corporate leaders were just appeasing racist and sexist clients, it implies that they held the belief that those within their own social stratum had prejudiced attitudes. As demonstrated by both the train and airline cases, once a job becomes associated with a specific race-gender, that linkage is likely to remain even after the clientele has become less elite.

The historical roots of all three instances demonstrate that, in the absence of legislation against discrimination, privileged White males have established a workplace structure that favors and promotes their own group. It should not be anticipated that, when left to their own devices, employers will construct systems devoid of race-gender considerations. The allocation of labor positions such as pilot, porter, conductor, and flight attendant was not determined by the market's "invisible hand." Rather, the allocation of opportunities was contingent upon preexisting perceptions on racial, ethnic, and gender distinctions.

Furthermore, companies within the railroad and aviation sectors allocated substantial financial resources toward the litigation of legal proceedings aimed at preserving discriminatory policies preventing porters from advancing to the position of conductors. In aviation, corporate officials made the decision to allocate additional resources toward legal proceedings in order to defend their numerous discriminatory practices, such as those pertaining to age, marital status, pregnancy, and appearance regulations, against flight attendants. The employment selections were not exclusively driven by the rationale of cost reduction and obtaining the most inexpensive workforce accessible. The restricted tenure of flight attendants, due to age and marriage limits imposed by airline executives, resulted in excessive expenditures on recruitment and training as a consequence of the continuous turnover of employees.

The labor systems devised by corporate executives embody and perpetuate social inequalities based on rank, ethnicity, and gender, while also highlighting the varying levels of importance assigned to the family lives of different worker groups. From an optimistic perspective, it might be argued that the seeming "natural" hierarchies based on race, gender, and ethnicity are neither inherent nor preset. The transformation of deeply established systems of inequity is possible.

In summary, significant findings from this research are that employers explicitly categorized workers according to race and gender in the workplace. Historically, there has been a pattern of employers engaging in discriminatory practices against individuals belonging to racial minority groups and women, with a particular emphasis on women of color. These discriminatory actions were prevalent both before and in situations where White male workers did not assert their demands or engage in unionization attempts. Furthermore, the determinants of companies' hiring decisions were not just influenced by labor market demographics or the availability of the labor pool. Once a decision of race-gender type for a job was made, employers demanded workers to exhibit a particular sort of subservience.

The hegemony of White masculinity was consistently upheld in part by excluding White men from the bottom of the workplace hierarchy and failing to develop any rationale as to why they were "naturally suited" for servitude. This system also places White men in positions of authority relative to other workers. In some instances, White male workers are socially on par with their customers. The cases discussed demonstrate that employers' efforts to create and uphold racial and gender hierarchies in the workplace are inextricably linked to their profit-seeking motives. It was through ideologies of race, ethnicity, gender, and nation that employers mediated their treatment of different workers as they sought to garner more profits.

THE JOURNEY

A great deal has changed between the late 1860s and today. As a result of over a century and a half of activism, labor organizing, lawsuits, marches, sit-ins, bloodshed, and protests, employers are no longer lawfully allowed to explicitly exclude people from an occupation on the basis of their race, gender, or nation of origin. There has been a remarkable amount of civic, social, and symbolic advancements that would have simply been unimaginable fifty years ago were it not for the agitation and sacrifice of those that came before us. Although beyond the scope of this book, the literature on the community and labor organizing of Pullman porters, especially *Pullman Porters and the Rise of Protest Politics in Black America, 1925–1945* by Beth Tompkins Bates, is highly recommended. My first trip to the Pullman Company archives at the Newberry Library in Chicago occurred shortly after President Barack Obama's first presidential election campaign. After a nonstop train journey that followed Abraham Lincoln's famous path across the chilly mid-Atlantic region and brought the incoming president one step closer to his inauguration, Barack Obama arrived in Washington. Obama was greeted by cheering crowds as he traveled from Philadelphia to Washington, D.C., braving the bitter cold. In three days, he would become president of the United States. Juxtaposing a porter's disciplinary files that fired him for "thinking he is as good as a White man" with Obama's train journey to the presidency was especially poignant. I wondered what the tens of thousands of porters that came before would have thought about the prospect of a Black president.

As for the aviation industry, the organizing efforts of flight attendants are chronicled extensively in various works. *Femininity in Flight* by Kathleen Barry provides an exhaustive analysis of the origins of labor and social activism among flight attendants. As a result of their organizing, significant strides have been made in eliminating the most flagrantly sexist and degrading aspects of the jobs. However, the vestiges of employers' initial decisions in the 1930s to link the stewardess job to White womanhood and piloting to White masculinity continue to resonate almost a century later. Louwanda Evan's *Cabin Pressure: African American Pilots, Flight Attendants, and Emotional Labor* carefully and expansively demonstrates the ongoing challenges faced by Black workers in this industry. Furthermore, 2022 data from the Bureau of Labor Statistics (BLS) demonstrate that among flight attendants: 70 percent are women, 78 percent are White, 11 percent are Black, 6.5 percent are Asian, and 12.5 percent are Hispanic/Latinx. Among pilots/flight engineers: 9 percent are women, 96 percent are White, 3 percent are Black, 2 percent are Asian, and 10 percent are Hispanic/Latinx. In short, the original patterns of race-gender typing persist greatly, especially among pilots.

The COVID-19 pandemic laid bare the perils of being a cruise ship worker, as employees were trapped on the boat for months on end, often without pay. The harshness of crew members; labor on contemporary cruise ships embodies employers' dreams of a work environment free of unions, labor laws, and governmental oversight. Compared to their counterparts in the U.S. railroad and aviation industries, cruise ship workers are especially disadvantaged. The "flags of convenience" system and global labor pool mean that there isn't a "home country" to pressure into enacting labor policies that would benefit the crew.

The pandemic also galvanized many Delta flight attendants to organize their own union. The Delta Flight Attendant Union website states:

> Since we launched our campaign for AFA representation in November 2019, hundreds of Delta Flight Attendants have become activists, working every day to build our Flight Attendant union. We've had thousands of conversations about the challenges Flight Attendants face and the importance of a strong union. In 2020, we saw over and over the critical importance of having voice and legally-binding rights on the job. While Flight Attendants in unionized workplaces had clear processes and procedures, management at Delta issued top-down directives that often created confusion and chaos with everything from scheduling to commuter rights to expectations of mask policy enforcement.

Although the fledgling union is not challenging the race-gender inequalities at work, there is ample evidence from recent scholarship that demonstrates that employers continue to play a significant role in workplace hierarchies.

EMPLOYERS AND CONTEMPORARY RACE-GENDER INEQUALITY

In all three cases examined in this book, employers were mostly exempt from antidiscrimination laws. In the post–Civil Rights era, it is illegal for a boss to discriminate against an employee on the basis of race, gender, or ethnicity. However, there is a vibrant field of contemporary scholarship that examines and explains how and why race-gender inequality persists in the workplace. This section reviews some of that literature.

The preeminence of White masculinity in the workplace has been weakened, but it persists. For example, despite a potential decline in their overall influence, White men are the prevailing cohort within the corporate upper echelons. This assertion is substantiated by statistical data, which reveals that in the year 2000, White males occupied a staggering 96.4 percent of cheif executive officer (CEO) positions within the esteemed Fortune 500 companies. Remarkably, even in the year 2020, they continue to maintain a significant majority, with a notable 85.8 percent representation.

Furthermore, it is worth noting that the majority of seats relinquished by White males were subsequently occupied by White females. Currently, White females account for a mere 6.8 percent of individuals holding CEO positions. Consequently, White people continue to dominate the Fortune 500 CEO landscape, representing 92.6 percent of the total. Merely 1 percent of the CEOs inside the Fortune 500 companies are individuals of African American descent, whereas 2.4 percent of CEOs are of East Asian or South Asian origin, and 3.4 percent are of Latinx background (Zweigenhaft 2020).

On the other end of the spectrum, White men with only a high school diploma fare better than their peers. The median earnings of those who completed high school were—White men ($41,800), Asian men ($39,200), Hispanic/Latinx men ($37,700), and Black men earned $35,000 in yearly income (National Center for Education Statistics 2023). Deirdre Royster's *Race and the Invisible Hand* is especially important for understanding the process whereby Black and White boys with similar grades in high school have disparate outcomes based on teachers' employment recommendations.

Contemporary scholarship demonstrates that employers' race-gender ideology continues to shape workplace hierarchies. In the field of economics, there are two predominant understandings of employers' propensity to discriminate. Becker's "irrational taste for discrimination" perspective asserts that people discriminate when they are willing to pay a price to limit their interactions and/or association with an undesirable group (Becker 1971). In other words, employers are willing to forgo maximizing profits and pay an economic price for their racism. The "statistical discrimination" perspective assumes employers have limited information about each individual they might hire. Therefore, bosses use stereotypes about the wider group to make a judgment about the individual.

> The employer who seeks to maximize expected profit will discriminate against Blacks or women if he believes them to be less qualified, reliable, long-term, etc., on the average than Whites and men, respectively, and if the cost of gaining information about the individual applicants is high. Skin color or sex is taken as a proxy for relevant data not sampled. (Phelps 1972, 659)

The statistical discrimination model helps explain how racial and gender discrimination can persist even in the absence of employers holding racist and/or sexist beliefs themselves.

Moving beyond the explicit or implicit biases of the employer, Pager and Small convincingly argue that "institutional discrimination can take at least two forms, organizational and legal, and that in both forms the decisions of a contemporary actor to discriminate, whether out of animus or statistical averaging, can be immaterial." Furthermore, as demonstrated in this book, "institutional discrimination is a vehicle through which past discrimination (intentional or not) has contemporary consequences" (Pager and Small 2020, 64).

Other sociologists have utilized various methods and contexts to explore the relationship between employers and race-gender inequities at work. For example, examining predominantly White spaces, Wingfield and Alston argue that employers expect workers of color to engage in "racial tasks" and be assigned to tasks and occupational roles that uphold the racial status quo (Wingfield and Alston, 2014). In addition to theoretical expositions, scholars have utilized experiments to demonstrate the relationship between race and employment prospects. For example, in their work, *Are Emily and Greg More Employable than Lakisha and Jamal* (2004), Bertrand and Mullainathan utilize field experiments to demonstrate that race continues to play a role in hiring prospects. In response to "help wanted" ads, their study created resumes that were randomly assigned Black- or White-sounding names. They found that White names receive 50 percent more callbacks for interviews. This disparity in callbacks was consistent across occupational categories, job industries, and the size of the business. Other incredibly rigorous research studies have also found racial discrimination in hiring and employment, even when employers claim otherwise (Bendick 2007; Bendick and Cohn 2021; Cohn 2019; Gaddis 2015; Moss and Tilly 2001; Pager and Quillian 2005; Quillain et. al 2017). Of particular importance to future employment patterns, a growing body of literature also discusses the socially constructed nature of skills. Warhurst, Tilly, and Gatta (2017) provide a comprehensive review of the literature regarding how the worker's race, gender, and class shape how employers define and remunerate perceived skills across various occupations.

In their groundbreaking book *Stories Employers Tell*, Moss and Tilly provide an amazingly comprehensive and detailed study of employers' practices and attitudes around race-gender by utilizing a wide-ranging survey of employers in Atlanta, Boston, Detroit, and Los Angeles. The authors conducted in-depth interviews with employers to explore the rationale, reasons, and beliefs that undergird their hiring decisions;. Moss and Tilly demonstrate that an employer's perception of a person's suitability for a particular job is shaped by racial and cultural stereotypes. For example, employers' race-gender ideology negatively impacts their assessments of Black men and single Black mothers as suitable employees. Migrant workers are deemed to be particularly suited to low-wage, manual labor jobs because they are deemed to be hard-working. This work is especially important because it demonstrates that employers' perceptions of skills and merit are inextricably linked with their ideas about race, class, and neighborhoods.

Most recently, Misra and Walters's book "Walking Mannequins" is an excellent examination of race-gender in the clothing retail sector, utilizing ethnographic observations and detailed interviews with workers. Their work makes clear that retail employers, like airline executives before them, reproduce racist and sexist "beauty" standards by attempting to regulate the appearance of their employees. Furthermore, race-gender hierarchies are reproduced through an elaborate system of surveillance and repeated interactions with management, coworkers, and customers (Misra and Walters 2022). This rich body of scholarship demonstrates there is no singular cause for race-gender inequality in this context; rather, it is an interlocking system and various patterns of behavior that produce unequal outcomes.

Whatever the causes, the impact of these forms of stratification continues to resonate societally. The persistence of race, ethnic, and gender enclaves in lower-status jobs is evidenced by various data points. For example, BLS data from 2022 shows that half of maids/housekeepers are Latinas. Similar to the porters before them, many room cleaners, maids, and food service workers are low-paid and reliant on tips. The system of gratuities further reflects the devaluation of their labor. For example, an online article in U.S. News titled "The Ultimate Guide to Tipping" suggests tipping wait staff at a sit-down restaurant 20 percent of the bill. For hotel housekeeping, they recommend "about $3 to $5 for the initial service and then $1 to $3 per night after that" (LaPonsie and Hogan, 2023). In short, a $200 dinner at an elegant restaurant garners a $40 tip for the waiter. Compare this to the $3–5 suggested for the person who scrubs the toilet and shower, mops and vacuums the floors, changes the bedding and towels, and inhales fumes from powerful cleaning agents. The devaluation speaks for itself.

This book illuminates how systems of inequality are undergirded by a story, a narrative to justify and explain why some humans are deserving of servitude from others. The legitimation of inequality can take the form of classism, racism, sexism, nationalism, religion, or the claim of meritocracy. If we seek to undermine systems of inequality, we need to deconstruct the ideological beliefs that justify stratification.

Employers in the railroad and airline industries did not relent in demanding racist and sexist performances from their employees until organized and individual workers demanded dignity and better conditions. Furthermore, the organizing of workers was shaped by and influenced by wider activism around race and gender. Specifically, the "New Negro" movement of the 1920s (Bates-Tompkins, 1996) and the second-wave feminism (Barry, 2007). One of the most important lessons derived from studying the Pullman porters and flight attendants is that employers only conceded and improved conditions after unrelenting organizing and resistance on the part of workers. Both porters and flight attendants demanded that employers eliminate the most degrading and demeaning parts of their jobs. Although outside the scope of this book, it is crucial that readers understand that only through organizing and challenging prevailing racial and gender ideologies, were both groups of workers ultimately able to secure more dignity in the workplace.

The percentage of workers represented by a union remains stagnant at approximately 10 percent of the workforce, and labor laws in the United States make it immensely onerous to form a union. Notwithstanding these challenges, the past few years have seen an upsurge in labor organizing both inside and outside the formal union structure. Rail workers, flight attendants, maids/housekeepers, restaurant workers, and pilots have all been represented in this current wave. Reading the monthly edition of *Labor Notes* makes clear that within and outside the boundaries of a formal union, domestic workers, writers, students, teachers, baristas at Starbucks, delivery drivers, Amazon sorters, nursing home attendants, sex workers, actors, programmers, and countless other workplaces are being organized with varying degrees of success.

Attending the most recent gathering of Labor Notes, it is enlivening to see a new, incredibly diverse generation of labor activists, many of whom are working at the intersection of worker rights and other social movements such as immigrant rights, racial justice, disability activism, LGBTQ and reproductive rights, education reform, and sustainability. These workers contend that it is possible, indeed necessary, to understand race-, gender-, and national-based structures of inequality among laborers while simultaneously working toward their shared material interests as workers demanding that employers render them greater remuneration, autonomy, control, and dignity in the workplace. I certainly hope they succeed.

References

Acker, Joan. "Hierarchies, jobs, bodies: A theory of gendered organizations." *Gender & Society* 4, no. 2 (1990): 139–158.

Allen, Theodore W. *The Invention of the White Race*. Verso, 1994.

____*The Invention of the White Race, Volume 2: The Origin of Racial Oppression in Anglo-America*. National Geographic Books, 2012.

Amott, Teresa L., and Julie A. Matthaei. *Race, Gender, and Work: A Multi-Cultural Economic History of Women in the United States*. South End Press, 1996.

Anderson, C.F. *Freemen Yet Slaves under "Abe" Lincoln's Son*. Press of the Enterprise Printing House, 1904.

Arnesen, Eric. *Waterfront Workers of New Orleans: Race, Class, and Politics, 1863–1923*. University of Illinois Press, 1994.

_____*Brotherhoods of Color: Black Railroad Workers and the Struggle for Equality*. Harvard University Press, 2009.

Asher, Robert, and Charles Stephenson. *Labor Divided: Race and Ethnicity in United States Labor Struggles, 1835–1960*. SUNY Press, 1990.

Barry, Kathleen. *Femininity in Flight: A History of Flight Attendants*. Duke University Press, 2007.

Bates, Beth Tompkins. *Pullman Porters and the Rise of Protest Politics in Black America, 1925–1945*. Univ of North Carolina Press, 2001.

Becker, Gary S. *The Economics of Discrimination, Chicago*. University of Chicago Press, 1971.

Bendick, Jr, Marc. "Situation testing for employment discrimination in the United States of America." *Horizons Stratégiques* 3, (2007): 17–39.

Bendick Jr, Marc, and Elias M. Cohn. "Race discrimination and segregation in manufacturing jobs: Evidence from matched-pair testing of staffing agencies." *The Social Science Journal* 58, (2021): 1–17.

Berman, Edward. "The Pullman Porters win." *The Nation* 141, no. 3659 (1935): 217.

Bertrand, Marianne, and Sendhil Mullainathan. "Are Emily and Greg more employable than Lakisha and Jamal? A field experiment on labor market discrimination." *American Economic Review* 94, no. 4 (2004): 991–1013.

Blauner, Robert. *Racial Oppression in America*. Harper Collins College Div, 1972.

Bonacich, Edna. "A theory of ethnic antagonism: The split labor market." *American Sociological Review* 37, (1972): 533–547.

____"Advanced capitalism and black/white race relations in the United States: A split labor market interpretation." *American Sociological Review* 41, (1976): 34–51.

____"The past, present, and future of split labor market theory." *Research in Race and Ethnic Relations* 1, no. 1 (1979): 17–64.

Bonilla-Silva, Eduardo. "Rethinking racism: Toward a structural interpretation." *American Sociological Review* 62, (1997): 465–480.

Boswell, Terry, Cliff Brown, and John Brueggemann. *Racial Competition and Class Solidarity*. SUNY Press, 2006.

Brattain, Michelle. *The Politics of Whiteness: Race, Workers, and Culture in the Modern South*. Princeton University Press, 2001.

Brier, Stephen. "In defense of Gutman; The Union's case." *International Journal of Politics, Culture, and Society* 2, (1989): 382–395.

Brotherhood of Sleeping Car Porters. *Records of the Brotherhood of Sleeping Car Porters*. Holdings of the Chicago Historical Society and the Newberry Library, 1925–1969. https://www.lexisnexis.com/documents/academic/upa_cis/1550_RecsBroSleepCarPorSerAPt3.pdf.

Brown, Cliff. "The role of employers in split labor markets: An event-structure analysis of racial conflict and AFL organizing, 1917–1919." *Social Forces* 79, no. 2 (2000): 653–681.

Brown, Cliff, and Terry Boswell. "Strikebreaking or solidarity in the great steel strike of 1919: A split labor market, game-theoretic, and QCA analysis." *American Journal of Sociology* 100, no. 6 (1995): 1479–1519.

Browne, Irene, and Joya Misra. "The intersection of gender and race in the labor market." *Annual Review of Sociology* 29, no. 1 (2003): 487–513.

Buder, Stanley. "Pullman: an Experiment in Industrial Order and Community Planning, 1880–1930." PhD diss., The University of Chicago, 1966.

Carlisle, Rodney P. *Sovereignty for Sale: The Origins and Evolution of the Panamanian and Liberian Flags of Convenience*. Naval Institute Press, 1981.

Carnival Corporation, Annual Report 2014. https://www.carnivalcorp.com/static-files/c830832f-1fc1-4cc0-8445-986b8b4ae582.

Carson, Jenny. "Riding the rails: Black railroad workers in Canada and the United States." *Labour/Le Travailleur* 50, (2002): 275–296.

Chapman, Paul K. *Trouble on Board: The Plight of International Seafarers*. ILR Press, 1992.

Chin, Christine B.N. "Labour flexibilization at sea: 'MINI U [NITED] N [ATIONS]' CREW ON CRUISE SHIPS." *International Feminist Journal of Politics* 10, no. 1 (2008a): 1–18.

____*Cruising the Global Economy: Profits, Pleasure, and Work at Sea*. Ashgate, (2008b).

Cohn, Samuel. *Race, Gender, and Discrimination at Work*. Routledge, 2019.

Collins, Patricia Hill. *Black Feminist Thought: Knowledge, Consciousness, and the Politics of Empowerment*. Routledge, 2022.

Coons, Lorraine, and Alexander Varias. *Steamship Travel in the Interwar Years: Tourist Third Cabin*. Amberley Publishing Limited, 2016.

Cox, Oliver Cromwell. *Caste, Class, & Race*. Naval Institute Press, 1948.

Creasman, Kim. "Black Birds in the sky: The legacies of Bessie Coleman and Dr. Mae Jemison." *The Journal of Negro History* 82, no. 1 (1997): 158–168.

Crenshaw, Kimberlé. "Demarginalizing the intersection of race and sex: A black feminist critique of antidiscrimination doctrine, feminist theory and antiracist politics." In *Feminist Legal Theories*, edited by Karen Maschke, pp. 23–51. Routledge, 2013.

Cruise Lines International Association (CLIA). *2022 Cruise Industry Outlook*. CLIA, 2023.

Derickson, Alan. ""Asleep and awake at the same time": Sleep denial among Pullman Porters." *Labor: Studies in Working-Class History of the Americas* 5, no. 3 (2008): 13–44.

Dickinson, Bob, and Andy Vladimir. *Selling the Sea: An Inside Look at the Cruise Industry*. Wiley, 2008.

Dorman, James H. "The strange career of Jim Crow Rice (with apologies to Professor Woodward)." *Journal of Social History* 3, no. 2 (1969): 109–122.

Douglas, Deborah G. *American Women, and Flight since 1940*. University Press of Kentucky, 2004.

Draper, Alan. *Conflict of Interests: Organized Labor and the Civil Rights Movement in the South, 1954–1968*. Cornell University Press, 1994.

Du Bois, W. E. B. *Black Reconstruction in America 1860–1880: An Essay Toward a History of the Part Which Black Folk Played in the Attempt to Reconstruct Democracy in America*, Antheneum, [1935]1993.

____*Darkwater: Voices from within the Veil*. Schocken Books, 1969.

Duffy, Mignon. "Doing the dirty work: Gender, race, and reproductive labor in historical perspective." *Gender & Society* 21, no. 3 (2007): 313–336.

Esch, Elizabeth. *The Color Line and the Assembly Line: Managing Race in the Ford Empire*. Vol. 50. Univ of California Press, 2018.

Evans, Louwanda. *Cabin Pressure: African American Pilots, Flight Attendants, and Emotional Labor*. Rowman & Littlefield, 2013.

Feagin, Joe, and Kimberley Ducey. *Elite White Men Ruling: Who, What, When, Where, and How*. Routledge, 2017.

Feagin, Joe R. *The White Racial Frame: Centuries of Racial Framing and Counter-Framing*. Routledge, 2020.

Foner, Philip Sheldon. *Organized Labor and the Black Worker, 1619–1981*. International Publishers, 1982.

Foner, Philip S., and Ronald L. Lewis, *The Black Worker: A Documentary History from Colonial Times to the Present*. Temple University, 1981.

Gaddis, S. Michael. "Discrimination in the credential society: An audit study of race and college selectivity in the labor market." *Social Forces* 93, no. 4 (2015): 1451–1479.

Garin, Kristoffer A. *Devils on the Deep Blue Sea: The Dreams, Schemes, and Showdowns that Built America's Cruise-Ship Empires*. Penguin, 2006.

Glenn, Evelyn Nakano. *Unequal Freedom: How Race and Gender Shaped American Citizenship and Labor*. Harvard University Press, 2002.

Goffman, Erving. *Asylums: Essays On the Social Situation of Mental Patients and Other Inmates*. Aldine Pub. Co, 1962.

Green, Lorenzo, and Carter Woodson. *The Negro Wage Earner*. The Association for the Study of Negro Life and History, 1930.

Greenberg, Stanley B. *Race and State in Capitalist Development: Comparative Perspectives*. Yale University Press, 1980.

Grossman, James R. *Land of Hope: Chicago, Black Southerners, and the Great Migration*. University of Chicago Press, 1989.

Gutman, Herbert George. *The Negro and the United Mine Workers of America: The Career and Letters of Richard L. Davis and Something of their Meaning, 1890–1900*. Random House, 1968.

Halpern, Rick. *Down on the Killing Floor: Black and White Workers in Chicago's Packinghouses, 1904–54*. University of Illinois Press, 1997.

Halpern, Rick, and Roger Horowitz. *Meatpackers: An Ōral History of Black Packinghouse Workers and their Struggle for Racial and Economic Equality*. NYU Press, 1999.

Hartmann, Heidi I. "The family as the locus of gender, class, and political struggle: The example of housework." *Signs: Journal of Women in Culture and Society* 6, no. 3 (1981): 366–394.

Harris, Cheryl I. "Whiteness as property." *Harvard Law Review* (1993): 1707–1791.

Hill, T. Arnold. "The Negro in industry." *American Federationist* 32, (1925): 915–920.

Hill, Herbert. "Racial discrimination in the nation's apprenticeship training Programs." *Phylon (1960-)* 23, no. 3 (1962): 215–224.

____"Racial inequality in employment: The patterns of discrimination." *The Annals of the American Academy of Political and Social Science* 357, no. 1 (1965): 30–47.

____"Race and ethnicity in organized labor: The historical sources of resistance to affirmative action." *Journal of Intergroup Relations* 12, no. 4 (1984): 5–50.

____"Myth-making as labor history: Herbert Gutman and the United mine workers of America." *International Journal of Politics, Culture, and Society* 1, (1988): 132–200.

____"The problem of race in American labor history." *Reviews in American History* 24, no. 2 (1996): 189–208.

____"Race and the steelworkers union: White privilege and black struggles." *New Politics* 8, no. 4 (2002): 8–10.

Hirsch, Susan E. *After the Strike: A Century of Labor Struggle at Pullman*. U of Nebraska Press, 2003.

Hochschild, Arlie Russell. *The Managed Heart: Commercialization of Human Feeling*. Univ of California Press, 2012.

Horowitz, Roger. *Negro and White, Unite and Fight!: A Social History of Industrial Unionism in Meatpacking, 1930–90*. University of Illinois Press, 1997.

Husband, Joseph. *The Story of the Pullman Car*. A.C. McClurg and Co, 1917.

Ignatiev, Noel. *How the Irish became White*. Harvard University, 1994.

ITF. *Sweatships: What it's Really Like to Work on Board Cruise Ships*. War on Want and International Transport Workers Federation, 2002.

Jacobson, Matthew Frye. *Whiteness of a Different Color*. Harvard University Press, 1999.

James, Winston. *Holding aloft the Banner of Ethiopia: Caribbean Radicalism in Early Twentieth-Century America*. Verso, 1998.

Jolly-Ryan, Jennifer. "Chipping away at discrimination at the country club." *Pepperdine Law Review* 25, (1997): 495.

Kessler-Harris, Alice. *Out to Work: A History of Wage-Earning Women in the United States*. Oxford University Press, 1982.

____*A Woman's Wage: Historical Meanings and Social Consequences*. University Press of Kentucky, 1990.

Kirshenman, Joleen, and Kathryn M. Neckerman. "We'd love to hire them, but…": The meaning of race for employers." In *Race and ethnic conflict*, edited by Fred L. Pincus, pp. 152–161. Routledge, 2019.

Klein, Ross. *Cruise Ship Blues: The Underside of the Cruise Industry*. New Society Publishers, 2002.

Laponsie, Maryaline, and Hogan, Colin. "The ultimate guide to tipping." *US News*. 2023. https://money.usnews.com/money/personal-finance/articles/tipping-etiquette-101.

Laslett, Barbara, and Johanna Brenner. "Gender and social reproduction: Historical perspectives." *Annual Review of Sociology* 15, no. 1 (1989): 381–404.

Letwin, Daniel. *The Challenge of Interracial Unionism: Alabama Coal Miners, 1878–1921*. Univ of North Carolina Press, 1998.

Lichtenstein, Alex. "Racial conflict and racial solidarity in the Alabama coal strike of 1894: New evidence for the Gutman-Hill debate." *Labor History* 36, no. 1 (1995): 63–76.

Marks, Carole. "Split labor markets and black-white relations, 1865-1920." *Phylon (1960-)* 42, no. 4 (1981): 293–308.

May, Martha. "The historical problem of the family wage: The Ford motor company and the five dollar day." *Feminist Studies* 8, no. 2 (1982): 399–424.

McKiven Jr, Henry M. *Iron and Steel: Class, Race, and Community in Birmingham, Alabama, 1875–1920*. University of North Carolina Press, 2011.

Meier, August, and Elliott M. Rudwick. *From Plantation to Ghetto: An Interpretive History of American Negroes*. Hill & Wang, 1968.

Misra, Joya, and Kyla Walters. *Walking Mannequins: How Race and Gender Inequalities Shape Retail Clothing Work*. University of California Press, 2022.

Moss, Philip, and Chris Tilly. *Stories Employers Tell: Race, Skill, and Hiring in America*. Russell Sage Foundation, 2001.

Myers, Kristen A., and Passion Williamson. "Race talk: The perpetuation of racism through private discourse." *Race and Society* 4, no. 1 (2001): 3–26.

National Center for Education Statistics. "Annual earnings by educational attainment." *Condition of Education*. U.S. Department of Education, 2023.

Nelson, Bruce. *Divided We Stand: American Workers and the Struggle for Black Equality*. Princeton: Princeton University Press, 2001.

Nichols, T.L. *Forty Years of American Life*. Longmans, 1874.

Norrell, Robert J. "Caste in steel: Jim Crow careers in Birmingham, Alabama." *The Journal of American History* 73, no. 3 (1986): 669–694.

Omelia, Johanna, and Michael Waldock. *Come Fly with Us: A Global History of Flight Attendants*. Collectors Press, 2003.

Omi, Michael, and Howard Winant. *Racial Formation in the United States*. Routledge, 2014.

Owings, Alison. *Hey, Waitress!: The USA from the Other Side of the Tray*. Univ of California Press, 2002.

Pager, Devah, and Lincoln Quillian. "Walking the talk? What employers say versus what they do." *American Sociological Review* 70, no. 3 (2005): 355–380.

Perata, David D. *Those Pullman Blues: An Oral history of the African American Railroad Attendant*. No. 22. Twayne Publishers, 1996.

Pettigrew, Thomas F. "New Black-White patterns: How best to conceptualize them?" *Annual review of Sociology* 11, no. 1 (1985): 329–346.

Phelps, Edmund S. "The statistical theory of racism and sexism." *The American Economic Review* 62, no. 4 (1972): 659–661.

Piore, Michael. *Notes for a Theory of Labor Market Stratification*. Massachusetts Institute of Technology (1972).

Posadas, Barbara M. "The hierarchy of color and psychological adjustment in an industrial environment: Filipinos, the Pullman company, and the brotherhood of sleeping car porters." *Labor History* 23, no. 3 (1982): 349–373.

Quillian, Lincoln, Devah Pager, Ole Hexel, and Arnfinn H. Midtbøen. "Meta-analysis of field experiments shows no change in racial discrimination in hiring over time." *Proceedings of the National Academy of Sciences* 114, no. 41 (2017): 10870–10875.

Reich, Michael. *Racial Inequality: A Political-Economic Analysis*. Vol. 4883. Princeton University Press, 1981.

Reich, Michael, David M. Gordon, and Richard C. Edwards. "A theory of labor market segmentation." *The American Economic Review* 63, (1973): 359–365.

Reiff, Janice L., and Susan E. Hirsch. "Pullman and its public: Image and aim in making and interpreting history." *The Public Historian* 11, no. 4 (1989): 99–112.

RCIR, United States. Commission on Industrial Relations. *Industrial Relations: Final Report and Testimony*. Vol. 10. US Government Printing Office, 1915.

Reskin, Barbara F. "The proximate causes of employment discrimination." *Contemporary Sociology* 29, no. 2 (2000): 319–328.

____"Modeling ascriptive inequality: From motives to mechanisms." *American Sociological Review* 68, no. 1 (2003): 1–21.

Robles, Frances. "Nobody cares about the little people." *New York Times*, June 25, 2021.

Roediger, David R. *The Wages of Whiteness: Race and the Making of the American Working Class*. Verso, 1999.

____*Working Toward Whiteness: How America's Immigrants Become White*. Perseus Books, 2005.

Roediger, David R., and Elizabeth D. Esch. "One symptom of originality: Race and the management of labour in the history of the United States." Historical Materialism 17, no. 4 (2009): 3–43.

_____*The Production of Difference: Race and the Management of Labor in US history*. Oxford University Press, 2012.

Roemer, John E. "Divide and conquer: Microfoundations of a Marxian theory of wage discrimination." *The Bell Journal of Economics* 10, (1979): 695–705.

Rollins, Judith. *Between Women: Domestics and their Employers*. Temple University Press, 1985.

Royster, Deirdre. *Race and the Invisible Hand: How White Networks Exclude Black Men from Blue-Collar Jobs*. Univ of California Press, 2003.

Rozen, Frieda. "Technological advances and increasing militance: Flight attendant unions in the Jet Age." *Drygulski Wright et al., Women, Work and Technology* 225 (1987): 99–100.

Ruchames, Louis, ed. *Racial Thought in America: From the Puritans to Abraham Lincoln*. Vol. 1. University of Massachusetts Press, 1969.

Rust, Daniel L. *Flying Across America*. University of Oklahoma Press, 2012.

Sandoval-Strauaz, A.K. *Hotels: An American History*. Yale University Press, 2007.

Santino, Jack. "Miles of smiles, years of struggle: The negotiation of black occupational identity through personal experience narrative." *The Journal of American Folklore* 96, no. 382 (1983): 393–412.

____"A servant and a man, a hostess or a woman: A study of expressive culture in two transportation occupations." *Journal of American folklore* 99, (1986): 304–319.

____*Miles of Smiles, Years of Struggle: Stories of Black Pullman Porters*. University of Illinois Press, 1991.

Saxton, Alexander. "Blackface minstrelsy and Jacksonian ideology." *American Quarterly* 27, no. 1 (1975): 3–28.

Scott, Joan Wallach. "Gender: A useful category of historical analysis." *The American Historical Review* 91, no. 5 (1986): 1053–1075.

Small, Mario L., and Devah Pager. "Sociological perspectives on racial discrimination." *Journal of Economic Perspectives* 34, no. 2 (2020): 49–67.

Smith, Ryan A. "Race, gender, and authority in the workplace: Theory and research." *Annual review of sociology* 28, no. 1 (2002): 509–542.

Stainback, Kevin, Donald Tomaskovic-Devey, and Sheryl Skaggs. "Organizational approaches to inequality: Inertia, relative power, and environments." *Annual Review of Sociology* 36 (2010): 225–247.

Stephan, Nancy. "Race and gender: The role of analogy in Science." In *Anatomy of Racism,* edited by David Goldberg, pp. 38–57. University of Minnesota Press, 1990.

Spero, Sterling Denhard, and Abram Lincoln Harris. *The Black Worker: The Negro and the Labor Movement*. Atheneum, 1968.

Stewardess Story. *How to Become an Airline Stewardess*. http://www.stewardessstory.com/.

Stimpson, Steve. "Young women couriers." memo to A.G. Kinsman, passenger traffic manager at Boeing Air Transport, February 24, 1930. Steve Stimpson Collection, United Airlines Archives, Chicago.

____Speech delivered at the 25th Anniversary Stewardess Luncheon at the Ambassador Hotel in Los Angeles, Calif., on May 12, 1955.

____The Denver Post, December 26, 1962.

Stinchcombe, Arthur. "Organization-creating organizations." *Trans-action* 2, no. 2 (1965): 34–35.

Street, Paul. "The logic and limits of "plant loyalty": Black workers, white labor, and corporate racial paternalism in Chicago's stockyards, 1916–1940." *Journal of Social History* 29, (1996): 659–681.

Syriopoulos, Theodore, Michael Tsatsaronis, and Martha Gorila. "The global cruise industry: Financial performance evaluation." *Research in Transportation Business & Management* 45 (2022): 100558.

Terry, William C. "The perfect worker: Discursive makings of Filipinos in the workplace hierarchy of the globalized cruise industry." *Social & Cultural Geography* 15, no. 1 (2014): 73–93.

Tilly, Charles. *Durable Inequality*. University of California Press, 1998.

Tomaskovic-Devey, Donald. "The gender and race composition of jobs and the male/female, white/black pay gaps." *Social Forces* 72, no. 1 (1993): 45–76.

Tomaskovic-Devey, Donald, and Vincent J. Roscigno. "Racial economic subordination and white gain in the US South." *American Sociological Review* (1996): 565–589.

Tomaskovic-Devey, Donald, and Sheryl Skaggs. "An establishment-level test of the statistical discrimination hypothesis." *Work and Occupations* 26, no. 4 (1999): 422–445.

____"Sex segregation, labor process organization, and gender earnings inequality." *American Journal of Sociology* 108, no. 1 (2002): 102–128.

Tomaskovic-Devey, Donald, Melvin Thomas, and Kecia Johnson. "Race and the accumulation of human capital across the career: A theoretical model and fixed-effects application." *American Journal of Sociology* 111, no. 1 (2005): 58–89.

Trotter, Joe William. *Black Milwaukee: The making of an industrial proletariat, 1915–45*. University of Illinois Press, 1985.

____*Coal, Class, and Color: Blacks in Southern West Virginia, 1915–32*. University of Illinois Press, 1990.

Tuttle, William M. *Race Riot: Chicago in the Red Summer of 1919*. University of Illinois Press, 1996.

Tye, Larry. *Rising from the Rails: Pullman Porters and the Making of the Black Middle Class*. Macmillan, 2004.

U.S. Bureau of the Census. *Negroes in the United States, 1920–32*. U.S. Government Printing Office, 1935.

____*Historical Statistics of the United States, Colonial Times to 1970*. U.S. Government Printing Office, 1975.

Valien, Preston. "The brotherhood of sleeping car porters." *Phylon (1940–1956)* 1, no. 3 (1940): 224–238.

Vantoch, Victoria. *The Jet Sex: Airline Stewardesses and the Making of an American Icon*. University of Pennsylvania Press, 2013.

Wahba, Phil. "Carnival CEO Arnold Donald to step down, shrinking the already thin ranks of Black CEOs." *Fortune Magazine*, April 26, 2022.

Waldinger, Roger D. "Social Capital or Social Closure? Immigrant Networks in the Labor Market." In *UCLA:The Ralph and Goldy Lewis Center for Regional Policy Studies*. 1997. Retrieved from https://escholarship.org/uc/item/06z6331r.

Warhurst, Chris, Chris Tilly, and Mary Gatta. "A new social construction of skill." In *The Oxford handbook of skills and training*, edited by Warhurst, C., Mayhew, K., Finegold, D., and Buchanan, J., pp. 72–91. Oxford University Press, 2017.

Watkins-Owens, Irma. *Blood Relations: Caribbean Immigrants and the Harlem Community, 1900–1930*. Indiana University Press, 1996.

Weeden, Kim A. "Why do some occupations pay more than others? Social closure and earnings inequality in the United States." *American journal of sociology* 108, no. 1 (2002): 55–101.

Witz, Anne. "Patriarchy and professions: The gendered politics of occupational closure." *Sociology* 24, no. 4 (1990): 675–690.

Whitelegg, Drew. *Working the Skies: The Fast-Paced, Disorienting World of the Flight Attendant*. NYU Press, 2007.

Wingfield, Adia Harvey, and Renée Skeete Alston. "Maintaining hierarchies in predominantly White organizations: A theory of racial tasks." *American Behavioral Scientist* 58, no. 2 (2014): 274–287.

Yano, Christine R. *Airborne Dreams: "Nisei" Stewardesses and pan American world airways*. Duke University Press, 2011.

Zhao, Minghua. "Emotional labour in a globalised labour market: Seafarers on cruise ships." [Working Paper]. *School of Social Sciences Working Papers Series*, vol. 27. Cardiff: Cardiff University, 2002.

Zweigenhaft, Richie. "Fortune 500 CEOs, 2000-2020: Still male, still white." *The Society Pages*, October 2020. https://thesocietypages.org/specials/fortune-500-ceos-2000-2020-still-male-still-white/.

Index

African Americans, 3–4, 6–8, 12, 21, 26, 53; at bottom of social ladder, 53; in Chicago area, 50; males, 115; as reserve labor force, 6; within secondary (inferior) labor market sector, 8, 56; slavery and, 26; stewardesses, 94; Whites *versus*, 53; women, 95. *See also* Black workers
African Methodist Episcopal (AME) Church, 51
Ain't I a Woman (Truth), 13
airline industry (1910s–1970s), 2, 67–96; branding and marketing of flight attendant (1940s–1960s), 88–89; breaking, creating, and reinforcing race-gender norms (1930s–1960s), 83–86; emotional labor in, 80; federal government, role of, 68–69; flight attendants, 74; happenstance, role of, 75–78; lady pilots in, 70–72, 75; producing, marketing, and profiting from sexualization of stewardesses (1960s and 1970s), 90–92; reinforcing race-gender norms (1910s-1930s), 70–72; sexual purity in, 80–81; shut women out of cockpit (1930s), 72–74; tasks of flight attendants, 87–88; training women to "act like women" in, 83; transition from trains to airplanes, 67–96; from transporting mail to serving passengers, 69–70; upholding and surveilling beauty standards in, 81–82; war, piloting, and maintenance of hegemonic white masculinity, 87; White male stewards, 74–75; White women qualify to flight attendants, job requirements, 78–80; women of color in, 92–96
airmail service, 68–69
American Airlines, 79, 81
analytical strategy, 15–16
Anderson, C. F, 33
anti-Black racism, 37
Asian American women, 93, 96
Asian Femininity, 93

Banks, Patricia, 94–95
Baranowski, Peggy Lee, 82
Barnes, Jonathan L., 26
Barry, Kathleen, 118
Bates, Beth Tompkins, 117
Bates-Tompkins, 51
beauty standards (upholding and surveilling), flight attendants, 81–82
Birth of Nation, 21
Blackface minstrel, 53–55
Black jobs, 6

Black manhood, 2, 21, 32, 36–37
Black man's work, 3, 10, 19–22. *See also* porters/porters job
Black masculinity, 21
Blackness, 39
Black women, 17, 20, 35, 43, 48, 78, 92–96
Black workers, 3–4, 20–22; for "divide and conquer" strategy, 9–10; marginalization within occupational hierarchy, 6, 41; as public transport servants, 74; Pullman Company's employment of, 6; racial uplift of, 52–53; as reserve labor force, 6; super-exploitation of, 6; wealth, 6. *See also* African Americans; porters/porters job
Boeing Air Transport, 76–78
Bonacich, Edna, 3, 9–10
Borkland, C. R., 69
Boswell, Terry, 10
Bowen, James H., 24
Brown, Cliff, 10
Brueggemann, John, 10
Bureau of Labor Statistics (BLS), 118
busboys, 27

cabin boys, 74
Cabin Pressure: African American Pilots, Flight Attendants, and Emotional Labor (Evan), 118
cabin stewards, 105
café/food service attendants, 27
Capital Airlines, 95
capitalism, 1, 8
Carey, James, 51
Carnegie, Andrew, 25
Carnival Corporation, 99–100
Carry, E. F., 57
Car Service Rules from 1888, 30
Cartwright, Samuel A., 36–37
Central Transportation Company, 25–26
Chicago, 22
Chicago and Alton Railroad company, 23–24
Chicago River, 22
Chicago's Midway Airport, 72
Chin, B. N., 110–11
Church, Ellen, 75–77
CIO unions, 3–4
Civil Rights Act (1964), 95
Cochran, Jacqueline, 71
Coleman, Bessie, 71–72
Collins, Patricia Hill, 13
Combahee River Collective, 13
conductor job, 19, 21–22, 26, 39; 1915 monthly wage schedule for, 42; *versus* porters job, 41–66; as service workers, 46
Contract Air Mail Act of 1925, 69
COVID-19 pandemic, 118
Crenshaw, Kimberlé, 13
Cruise Lines International Association (CLIA), 100
Cruising in the Global Economy: Profits, Pleasure, and Work at Sea (Chin), 110–11
cultural images regarding race, 20

Daimler Airways, 74
data, 15
Davis, Angela, 13
Delmonico, 33
Delta Flight Attendant Union, 118
deskilling, 13
Dickinson, Bob, 102, 104–5, 108
"divide and conquer" theory: Black workers and, 9–10; Bonacich argument against, 9; challenging, 9–10; framework, 6–8; refining, 9–10; in ships, 112–14
domesticated otherness, 93
Doty, Duane, 35
Du Bois, W. E. B., 6–8, 14
Duncan, Charles C., 98

Earhart, Amelia, 71
Eastern Europeans, 111–12
Edwards, Richard C., 7–8
elite White men, 1–2
emotional labor, 80
employers: benefits from super-exploitation of Black workers, 6;

Bonacich theoretical stance regarding role of, 9–10; economic motivations, 9–10; exclusions in workforce, 5; laissez-faire attitude, 9; race-gender hierarchies in workforce, 1, 5, 17, 119–22; race-gender ideology, 2, 19–37, 41, 116; in racial discrimination, 6, 9–10, 19–37; racialized paternalism and, 10–11; role in spreading cultural images regarding race, 20; segregation in workforce, 5
enemy race, 93
enslaved people, 4
entertainment-service-transport sector, 1
Equal Employment Opportunity Commission (EEOC), 86
Evan, Louwanda, 118
executives, 16, 39–66; decision to exclude women from piloting, 72–74; minstrel, 53–55; on pensions, 43–44; race-gender ideology, 41, 44; race in private discourse between, 60–62; race in public discourse, 44
exotic geishas, 96

federal government, role for airline industry, 68–69
Federation Aeronautique Internationale in Paris, 72
Femininity in Flight (Barry), 118
feminization of labor, 57–60
Filipino men, 74, 109–11, 115
first-generation European immigrants, 4
first service workers, Pullman Company, 26–32
first sleeping cars, Pullman Company, 23–26
first workers, 98–99
flags of convenience system, 100–102
flight attendants, 74; Asian American women as, 93; beauty standards (upholding and surveilling), 81–82; branding and marketing (1940s–1960s), 88–89; emotional labor and, 80; sexually appealing but not sexually active, 89–90; sexual purity and, 80–81; tasks of, 87–88; training women to "act like women" for, 83; white women qualify to (job requirements), 78–80
floating resort, 100
Freemen Yet Slaves under "Abe" Lincoln's Son (Anderson), 33
Frontier Airlines, 73
Fun Ship, 99

geisha girls, 93, 115
gendered racialization, 2, 5, 17, 19–37, 41, 44, 116, 119–22
gendered systems of inequality, 12–13, 119–22
The Girl on the Pullman, 45
global labor force, 102
Goffman, Erving, 97
Gordon, David M., 7–8

happenstance, role of, 75–78
Hearst, William Randolph, 67–68
hegemony of White masculinity, 1–2, 73, 114, 117; in airline industry, 87; Black *versus*, 16–17; in Pullman Railroad Company, 16–17; ships/cruise industry, 114
hierarchical shipboard social system, 102–3
Hill, Herbert, 4
hiring practices, 2, 19, 74
How to Become an Airline Stewardess, 83
Hungerford, L. S., 41, 44

Ignatiev, Noel, 4
inequality: gendered systems of, 1–5, 11–13, 17, 20–22, 119–22; racialized systems of, 1–5, 11–13, 17, 20–22, 119–22
inertia, 20
International Transport Workers Federation (ITF), 102
intersectionality, 13
Irish immigrants, 4

Japanese American stewardesses, 93
jokes, racialized, 56–57

Kelly, M. Clyde, 69
Keys, Clement M., 70

labor market segmentation, 7–8
lady pilots, 70–72, 75–76
laissez-faire ideology, 9
Lake Michigan, 22
Lincoln, Abraham, 117
Lincoln, Robert Todd, 40, 43–44, 50, 52
Lindbergh, Charles, 70, 73–74
Love Boat, 99

Madison Avenue, 90
Mad Men, 88
majority paternalism, 11
Mardi Gras, 99
Marxist functionalism, 9
McKiven Jr, Henry M., 3
methods, 15
Michigan Central Railroad Company, 24
minority paternalism, 11
minstrel executives/managers, 53–54
modern cruise ship industry, 99–100
monopoly capitalism, 8

nation's business, 45–52
neo-Marxist theories, 9
new leadership, 114
Nichols, Ruth, 71
Nisei women, 93
non-Whites workers, 5; apprenticeships, exclude from, 5; on-the-job training, exclude from, 5; *versus* White workers, 5–10. *See also* Black workers
Norwegian Cruise Line Holdings, 100
Nyrop, Donald, 94

Obama, Barack, 117
oceanic travel for leisure, 98
oligopolistic corporations, 8
Omelia, Johanna, 90
opportunity hoarding at work, White workers in, 5
Ovington, Earl, 68

Pacific Islander women, 96
paddle-wheel ships, 98
Pan Am, 77, 92–93
Panama, ships/cruise industry in, 101–2
passengers, ships/cruise, 100
Patterson, William, 76
Pegler, Westbrook, 56
pensions, 43–44
people of color, 2. *See also* African Americans; Asian American women; Black women; Black workers
Pettigrew, Thomas F., 6
pin-up, 89
"Pioneer" sleeping car, 23–24
Piore, Michael, 7
porters/porters job, 6, 19, 26–38, 39–66, 105; 1915 monthly wage schedule for, 42; in advertising and popular culture, 44–45; benevolent-exploitative racialized paternalism, 50–52; *versus* conductor job, 41–43; feminization of, 57–60; pensions denied to, 43–44; publicly racialized, 44–45; racial ideology for, 39–40, 62–66; singing race and, 55; wages for, 40–43; as world's most perfect servant, 46–47
psychological wage, 4
Pullman, George, 16, 19; in Chicago, 22; first service workers, 26–32; first sleeping cars, 23–26; racial ideology, 19, 25–26, 39–40
Pullman Palace Car Company, 24–26
Pullman Porters and the Rise of Protest Politics in Black America, 1925-1945 (Bates), 117
Pullman Railroad Company (1858–1880s), 1, 15–17, 19–38; background of, 22–38; Black *versus* White masculinity, 16–17; Black-White

interaction, norms regarding, 27; charitable donations (1897–1913), 50; employment of Black men and porters, 6, 19, 26–38; executives, 16, 39–66; first service workers, 26–32; first sleeping cars, 23–26; in majority paternalism, 11; in minority paternalism, 11; monthly pensions of employees, 1904, 43–44; racial hierarchies in, 39; racial ideology, 19, 25–26, 39–40; Southside Chicago Black community, paternalism in, 51; surveillance system, 28–29
Pullman Southern Palace Car Company, 25–26

Queen Mary ship, 99

race-gender paternalism, 11
race-gender segregation in airline industry, 2, 5, 17
race-gender workplace inequality, 1–5, 11–13, 17, 20–22, 119–22
race/racism, 11, 115; cultural images regarding, 20; in private discourse between company executives, 60–62; in public discourse, 44; singing, 55
racial antagonism, 6–7
racial discord, 7
racial discrimination, employers in, 6, 9–10
racial disharmony, 7
racial-ethnic-gender-class ideologies, 20
racial formation, 4, 11
racial ideology, 15, 19; for porters job, 39–40, 62–66
racialization, 20; gendered, 2, 5, 17, 19–37, 41, 44, 116, 119–22; jokes, 56–57; paternalism, 10–11, 16, 39, 50–51; systems of inequality, 11–12
racial projects, 11
racial uplift of Blacks, 52–53
railroads, 22–23
Regulations for Porters and Conductors Approved 1872, 29
Reich, Michael, 7–8
Richey, Helen, 73
Rising from the Rails (Tye), 38
Roediger, David R., 4
Roemer, John E., 7
Rogers, Cal, 68
Royal Caribbean Cruise, 99–100

savages, 37
Schott, Henry, 45
second-generation European immigrants, 4
service workers, 98
sexism, 90–92, 115
sexualization of stewardesses (1960s and 1970s), 90–92
sexual purity, flight attendant, 80–81
ships/cruise industry, 97–98; crew members, 104–5; divide and conquer strategy and, 112–14; Eastern Europeans, case of, 111–12; economy, 100–101; Filipino men and, 109–11; first workers, 98–99; flags of convenience system, 100–102; gender dynamics of workforce, 108–9; global labor force, 102; hegemony of white masculinity and, 114; hierarchical structure of, 102–3; history of oceanic travel for leisure, 98; inequality among crewmembers, 107–8; modern, 99–100; new leadership and, 114; officers, staff, and crew, 102–4; paddle-wheel, 98; in Panama, 101–2; passengers, 100; salaries/vacation for select ship positions, 107; staff, 104; wages and reliance on gratuities of workers, 107; workers, 105–7
singing race, 55
Skaggs, Sheryl, 20
Sleeping Car Conductors' Union, 38
sleeping car porters, 27
Smith, J. Henry, 53–54
social closure, 5
South, Jim Crow, 27

split labor market theory, 3, 9–10
Stainback, Kevin, 20
Stimpson, Steve, 76–77
Stinson, Katherine, 68, 73
Stout Air Services, 75
super-exploitation of Black workers, 6

Taylor, Carol Ruth, 95
"A Theory of Labor Market Segmentation" (Reich, Gordon, and Edwards), 7–8
tipping, 37, 40, 43, 75, 107, 121
Titanic ship, 99
Tomaskovic-Devey, Donald, 20
total institution, 97–98. *See also* ships
training, women to "act like women," 83
trains to airplanes, transition from, 67–96
Transcontinental Air Transport (TAT), 70, 75
Truth, Sojourner, 13
Twain, Mark, 98
Tye, Larry, 35, 38

Vantoch, Victoria, 76, 88–89
Vladimir, Andy, 105

Wabash YMCA, 50
wages, 40–43
Wages of Whiteness (Roediger), 4
Wagner Sleeping Car Company, 23
waiters, 105–6
Waldock, Michael, 90
war brides, 93
Warner, Emily, 73
wealth, 6
Wells, Mary, 91
West Indian, 63–64
White, Marlene, 94–95
White Americans, 4, 12, 21
White conductors, 19, 21–22, 26, 38, 46, 48
White femininity, 2, 67–96
White heteropatriarchy, 115
White male: attendants, 76; conductors, 19, 21–22, 26, 38, 46, 48; demographic, 115–16; economic advantages for, 5; employers, 2–3; executives, 65, 119; managers, 32; in "opportunity hoarding" at work, 5; as privileged workers, 5; skilled workers, 13; stewards, 74–75; workers, 13, 117
White manhood, 13
White man's work, 3, 10, 19. *See also* conductor job
White masculinity, hegemony of, 1–2, 73, 117
White neighborhoods, 4
Whiteness as management, 14–15
White race, 4–5
White Reconstruction in America (Du Bois), 6–7
White supremacy, 3–5, 39, 53
White womanhood, 70–71, 77, 83, 118
White women, 2, 13, 35–37, 78–80; qualify to flight attendant job, 78–80
White workers, 3–16; majority paternalism for, 11; in marginalization of Whites, 3–16; in militant trade unionism and strikes, 3; *versus* non-Whites workers, 5–10; in opportunity hoarding at work, 5; psychological wage, 4; racism, 3; in social closure, 5; as strikebreakers, 3
women: in airline industry, 67–96; exclude from piloting, 72–74; marginalization of, 12–13; White, 2, 13, 35–37, 78–80; workers, 5; to work on historic ships, 99
women of color in airline industry, 92–96
Woodruff Sleeping Car Company, 23
workers: gender identity of, 2; racial discrimination against, 6, 9–10; racial identity of, 2; White, 3–16
workplace race, 3–6
Wright, Edward H., 51

Yano, Christine, 93

About the Author

Francisca E. Oyogoa, PhD, is an associate professor of sociology and African-American studies at Bard College at Simon's Rock in Great Barrington, MA.

www.ingramcontent.com/pod-product-compliance
Lightning Source LLC
LaVergne TN
LVHW091625180625
814171LV00002B/199